As...

D0985567

...more than 135 years our
guidebooks have unlocked the secrets
of destinations around the world,
sharing with travellers a wealth of
experience and a passion for travel.

**Rely on Thomas Cook as your
travelling companion on your next trip
and benefit from our unique heritage.**

Thomas Cook **pocket** guides

OSLO

Ann Burgess & Tom Burgess

Thomas
Cook

Your travelling companion since 1873

Written by Ann Burgess & Tom Burgess, updated by Renata Rubnikowicz

Published by Thomas Cook Publishing
A division of Thomas Cook Tour Operations Limited
Company registration no. 3772199 England
The Thomas Cook Business Park, Unit 9, Coningsby Road,
Peterborough PE3 8SB, United Kingdom
Email: books@thomascook.com, Tel: +44 (0) 1733 416477
www.thomascookpublishing.com

Produced by Cambridge Publishing Management Limited
Burr Elm Court, Main Street, Caldecote CB23 7NU
www.cambridgepm.co.uk

ISBN: 978-1-84848-515-0

Series Editor: Karen Beaulah
Production/DTP: Steven Collins

Printed and bound in Spain by GraphyCems

Cover photography © Goran Bogicevic/Shutterstock.com

CONTENTS

SYMBOLS KEY

The following symbols are used throughout this book:

ⓐ address ☏ telephone ⓦ website address
🕒 opening times Ⓝ public transport connections

The following symbols are used on the maps:

🅸 information office		▪ point of interest	
✈ airport		○ city	
✚ hospital		○ large town	
🛡 police station		○ small town	
🚍 bus station		══ motorway	
🚆 railway station		── main road	
⛴ port		minor road	
Ⓜ T-bane		— railway	
✝ cathedral		- - international border	
❶ numbers denote featured cafés & restaurants			

Hotels and restaurants are graded by approximate price as follows:
£ budget price **££** mid-range price **£££** expensive

▶ *Oslo's City Hall*

INTRODUCING
Oslo

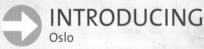

Introduction

A trip to Oslo offers something for everyone. The city itself is modern, while the surrounding scenery of the Oslofjorden and the wild woods and mountains of Nordmarka are beautiful. Oslo can be visited at any time of year, although the warmest and sunniest time to come is during the long days of summer. The whole city seems to live outdoors at this time, with restaurants, bars and museums keeping longer hours. Winter is also a lovely time to visit, particularly for those who enjoy skiing (both downhill and cross-country), luge, bobsleighing and skating. All of these sporting activities are within easy reach of the city centre, allowing you to spend your days in active pursuits and your evenings absorbing Oslo's cultural treasures.

Oslo was once home to playwright Henrik Ibsen, composer Edvard Grieg, violinist Ole Bull, artist Edvard Munch and sculptor Gustav Vigeland. The city is proud of its heritage and has kept alive its cultural traditions. And then of course there are the Vikings, those adventurous bad boys of the Dark to Middle Ages who were the first to scatter Norwegian traditions over a wide swathe of the globe. In later years they would be followed by the likes of Amundsen and Heyerdahl, continuing the tradition of exploration in a more socially responsible fashion.

Of Norway's most important museums, about 50 are based in Oslo. Among the most notable are the Munch Museum, the Fram Museum, the Norwegian Folk Museum the Vigeland Sculpture Park, the Viking Ship Museum and the Kon-Tiki Museum. Most of them are within walking distance of the city centre, or just a few minutes away by a very efficient public transport system.

History, art and culture abound in this vibrant capital city. Whatever your reasons for visiting Oslo, you won't be disappointed.

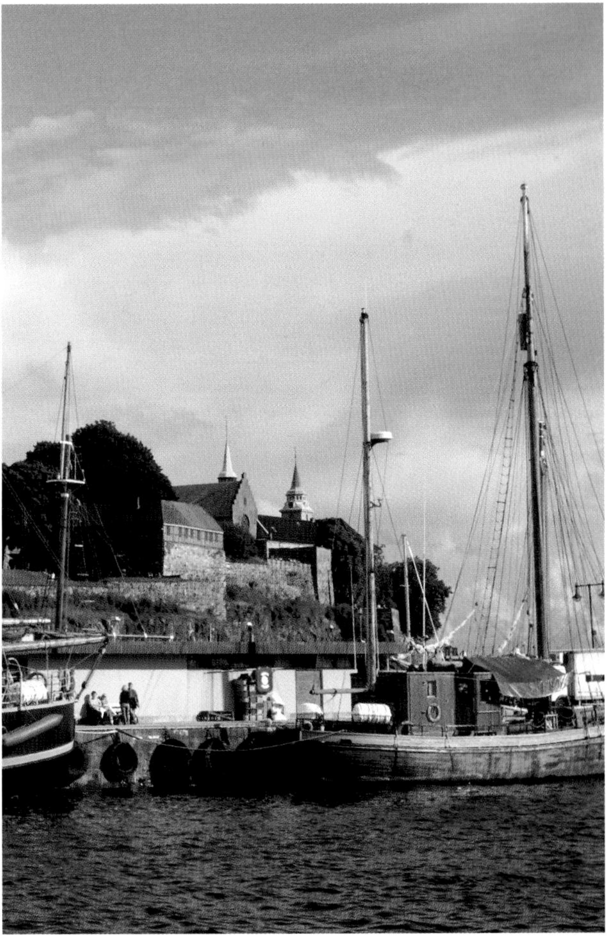

Akershus Slott has guarded Oslo harbour for centuries

When to go

SEASONS & CLIMATE

Oslo has four distinct seasons. Despite its northern latitude, the climate is quite moderate, owing to the effect of the Gulf Stream, which brings warm water from the Gulf of Mexico across the Atlantic and up the Norwegian coast. Summer temperatures average about 16°C (60°F), with highs that can reach 30°C (86°F), while winter temperatures average around 0°C (32°F), although they can go as low as –20°C (–4°F). You can expect about 80–90 mm (3–3 1/2 in) of rain in the summer months, and about 40–50 mm (1 1/2–2 in) in winter.

The main tourist season is from mid-June to mid-September. The summer season packs in a large number of festivals and other events, including plays and concerts, most of which are held outdoors. The city also has many parks and outdoor cafés where you can enjoy the long summer evenings. Visit Ⓦ www.visitoslo.com for more information about Oslo's summer activities.

If you're into winter sports, especially skiing, then Oslo makes a great winter destination. The first snows fall in late November or early December, and the skiing season gets into full swing at Christmas time, lasting until April. Oslo has many kilometres of cross-country ski runs and 14 alpine ski slopes within the city limits, and many more within easy reach. For more information on winter activities, see Ⓦ www.visitoslo.com

ANNUAL EVENTS
February
World Cup Biathlon Some of the world's best athletes gather in Oslo for Norway's number one annual ski event. Ⓦ www.biathlon-holmenkollen.no (Norwegian and German only)

March
Oslo International Church Music Festival Concerts are held in Oslo Cathedral and other churches within the city. ⓦ www.kirkemusikkfestivalen.no

Barnas Holmenkolldag The world's largest ski race for children, with about 9,000 children joining it at the traditional venue, Holmenkollen.

May–June
Syttende Mai (Constitution Day) Norway's national day is celebrated across the country on 17 May. Activities include children's parades and other festivities.

Norwegian Wood Rock Festival Mid-June sees this three-day festival featuring mostly Norwegian performers, but several international stars are usually on the programme, too. ⓦ www.norwegianwood.no

▲ *Colourful Constitution Day celebrations*

Oslo Middelalderfestival (Medieval Festival) A June festival that takes you back to the medieval ages, with concerts, theatre, a market and activities for children.

Oslo Gay & Lesbian Pride Week This festival takes place during the last week of June. Events include concerts, stand-up comedy, religious services, art exhibitions, photo workshops and bowling. Ⓦ www.skeivedager.no

Midsummer Night The evening of 23 June is the occasion for bonfires and celebrations throughout Norway. This is also the time when the OsloLive rock festival takes place over three or four nights at Akershus Fortress and in city-centre clubs. Ⓦ www.oslolivefestival.no

July–August

Summer at the Folk Museum The open-air museum puts on family activities such as traditional Norwegian dancing and food, and play sessions with the museum's animals.

Norway Cup The world's largest international football tournament for 12–19s is held during the first week of August. Ⓦ www.norwaycup.no

Oslo International Jazz Festival This major summer event takes place over a week in mid-August. All forms of jazz, from ragtime to rap, are showcased, with performers coming from all over the world to participate. Ⓦ www.oslojazz.no

Oslo Chamber Music Festival A mix of Norwegian and international musicians perform at various venues across the city in the middle of August. Ⓦ www.oslokammermusikkfestival.no

September–November

Ultima Contemporary Music Festival Held during September, this two-week festival sees local museums and theatres collaborating to stage the latest in music, dance and drama. Ⓦ www.ultima.no

Oslo International Film Festival Film lovers enjoy a combination of new trends and old classics in this 11-day event in November. Ⓦ www.oslofilmfestival.com

December
Nobel Peace Prize Award Parades and many other festivities are held in honour of the annual winner of the Nobel Peace Prize. Past performers have included Lionel Richie, Ellie Goulding, Andrea Bocelli and Diana Ross. Ⓦ www.nobelpeaceprize.org
Christmas Market Throughout December, the area in front of the City Hall becomes a large market where you can buy handcrafted Christmas presents and enjoy the holiday spirit. Ⓦ www.julemarked.no
Christmas Celebrations Christmas is celebrated with festivities and activities all over the city (see page 12).

PUBLIC HOLIDAYS
New Year's Day 1 Jan
Maundy Thursday, Good Friday & Easter Monday
28, 29 Apr & 2 May 2013, 17, 18 & 21 Apr 2014, 2, 3 & 6 Apr 2015
Labour Day 1 May
Constitution Day 17 May
Ascension Day 9 May 2013, 29 May 2014, 14 May 2015
Whit Monday (Pentecost) 20 May 2013, 9 May 2014, 25 May 2015
Christmas 25 & 26 Dec

On Public Holidays, public transport runs to Sunday schedules, and banks, post offices and public buildings are closed. Many shops (but not generally restaurants) also close.

Christmas in Oslo

A very special time of year in Norway, Christmas, or *Jul*, was originally a pagan fertility feast before becoming a Christian holiday. Similarly, an imaginary Viking gnome called *Nisse*, who traditionally brought good luck to pagan farmers, has morphed into a modern-day Santa Claus in the form of *Julenissen*. The lighting of the city's official Christmas tree at University Square on Karl Johans Gate, on the first Sunday of Advent, heralds the start of the holiday season in Oslo. The ice-skating rink in the city centre also opens at this time. For the whole of December Oslo is decked out in holiday lights and everyone is full of seasonal good spirits.

Pretty as the city centre may be, the holiday heart of Oslo is at the Norwegian Folk Museum on the Bygdøy Peninsula (see page 94), which plays host to a charming Christmas fair. Here you can create a gift in Santa's workshop, join carollers in song and attend a service in the old Stave Church. Interspersed among the museum's historic buildings are market stalls filled with crafts, decorations and seasonal foods.

You will also find traditional Christmas festivities at Bogstad Gård on the city outskirts (see page 100). The main manor building is decorated in the style of the 19th century, while the gift shop sells a range of unusual gifts. It's also worth stopping off for a seasonal bite to eat at the café.

In Oslo itself, a local sight to get into the holiday spirit is Bærums Verk, a 17th-century ironworks offering walks and horse-drawn sleigh rides (see page 100). The old workers' houses have been converted into small shops selling hand-blown glass, pottery and woven and knitted items. You can even try your hand at creating your own Christmas decorations.

○ *Pick up a traditional Christmas troll at a Christmas fair*

History

Although the history of Norway and its 'Norsemen' is a violent one, the history of Oslo itself is relatively quiet and peaceful. The Vikings had been plundering and pillaging for nearly 300 years by the time Oslo was founded in the mid-11th century by King Harald Hardråde. Roughly translated, Oslo means 'the pasture of the gods', from two Old Norse words, 'As', the Norse god, and 'lo', or 'field'.

By 1300 the city still had only 3,000 inhabitants, but it was nonetheless made the seat of the royal throne of King Haakon V, and consequently emerged as a centre of power. It was Haakon who started building Akershus Castle, which remains today. In 1349 the Black Death struck Norway, killing over half the country's population. Through royal marriages, Norway was joined to Denmark in 1380, with the Danes essentially ruling Norway for the next 400 years or so. Norway was a Catholic country until 1537, when the state religion became Evangelical Lutheran by royal decree. In 1624 Oslo was destroyed by fire. It was rebuilt by King Christian IV of Denmark, who renamed the city Christiania, after himself.

As a consequence of the Napoleonic Wars, Norway was ceded to Sweden in 1814, with Christiania officially becoming its capital. In 1877, the spelling of the city's name was changed to Kristiania, reverting to its original name of Oslo again in 1925.

In 1901 the Nobel Peace Prize was first awarded in Oslo. After years of struggle for independence, the union with Sweden was dissolved peacefully in 1905 and Norway became a fully democratic constitutional hereditary monarchy. Norway stayed out of World War I, although it lost half of its merchant fleet in the struggle. However, although Norway declared neutrality at the start of World War II, Germany invaded in 1940 and set up a puppet government under Vidkun Quisling. The exploits of the Norwegian resistance movement are legendary, and the execution of many Norwegian patriots took place in Akershus Castle. At the end of the war, the Germans surrendered to the Norwegian resistance movement at Akershus Castle, and Quisling was executed there.

Following the war, Oslo and the rest of Norway prospered. A strong fishing industry and the North Sea oil industry have kept the economy booming. Today Norway is one of the world's wealthiest nations per head of population. Although an active member of both NATO and the United Nations, to date an independently minded Norway has stayed out of the European Union with no immediate plans to join. The influx of immigrants from neighbouring European countries, Africa and Asia in recent years has given the country, and Oslo in particular, a more multicultural feel, with an increasingly international vibe. In July 2011 the attacks of a lone terrorist shocked the world, and Norwegians most of all. However, the country remains one of the world's safest destinations.

ST HALLVARD

The patron saint of Oslo is St Hallvard, a young Norwegian of royal descent who sacrificed his life in a deed of valour nearly 1,000 years ago. According to legend, Hallvard tried to save a pregnant woman fleeing assailants who had accused her of theft. He rowed her out into the fjord, but the pursuers caught and killed them both, put a millstone around Hallvard's neck, and sank his body. However, the body rose to the surface with the millstone still in place. This miracle led to Hallvard's canonisation. Today St Hallvard, shown holding a millstone in his right hand, is the main icon in the city of Oslo's coat of arms.

Lifestyle

Modern-day Norwegians enjoy one of the highest standards of living in the world. But it wasn't always so: a little over 50 years ago Norway was one of the poorest countries in Western Europe. This changed following the discovery of oil in the North Sea in the late 1960s, resulting in a spectacular reversal of economic fortune.

The Norwegians are a conundrum. They can be simultaneously independent and yet heavily reliant on government social programmes. They are curious about the world, but reluctant to join the European Union. Eminently fair-minded, but wary of strangers, Norwegians frequently even see themselves as a bundle of contradictions. But one thing almost all Norwegians have in common is their love of the outdoors. They take the *allemannsretten* or 'every man's right' very seriously. This is the rule that allows complete public access to wilderness lands. During the very short summer months there is a frenetic urge to engage in any and all kinds of outdoor activities. Of course, they also participate in these sports in winter, but it's precisely the long winter months that make Norwegians long for the summer sun.

Norwegians are also among the best-educated people on the planet. Education here is both compulsory and heavily funded. There is a wide range of programmes available to students, from traditional academic courses to vocational trades – and all of them are free. The citizens of Norway lead a very comfortable life. Although they are heavily taxed, they enjoy a vast range of benefits including free medical care, free university tuition, and a retirement pension. Because of the country's social programmes, with family allowances and generous parental leave policies, it is a good place to raise a family. The only fly in the ointment is the current problem of an ageing population.

Norway is a country with comparatively little external debt. Little wonder it can occasionally challenge world opinion, as in the case of its whaling policies. It will be interesting to see how Norway, which has spent only just over a century as a truly independent and sovereign nation, continues to evolve.

◆ *Norwegians love to get outside*

Culture

Oslo loves its museums, and with everything from art galleries to zoological gardens, they literally cover an A to Z of subjects. Architecture, children, literary heroes, skiers, sculptors and painters – they're all here. Still not enough? Don't worry: there are also historical museums, folk museums, geological museums and theatre museums. But these cultural repositories are more than just collections – they are a genuine reflection of Norwegian history, its life and its soul. The Viking Ship, Kon-Tiki and Fram Museums are authentic marvels. These are the

● The Vikings left some ships behind, now on show at the Viking Ship Museum

actual ships that sailed astonishing distances and made incredible discoveries: not replicas, the real thing. If you intend to sample as many of Oslo's museums as possible, invest in an Oslo Pass (see page 58).

Oslo is also a city of words. Literature has played a strong role in Norwegian culture. Few would dispute the impact and influence of Ibsen, Bjørnson or Sigrid Undset. Oslo is still a place that nurtures authors: Jostein Gaarder's powerful novel *Sophie's World* was a worldwide hit in the 90s, while recently crime writers such as Jo Nesbø and Karin Fossum have become worldwide bestsellers.

Art, too, is a very powerful influence in everyday Oslo. Art is everywhere in the city – not just in galleries but also on the streets, along the waterfront and in the parks. The sculpture park devoted

to the work of Gustav Vigeland and the museums dedicated to the work of Edvard Munch and other Norwegian artists help drive home the huge impact these artists had.

Music is big in Oslo. During the summer months concerts are held in parks and other open-air venues around the city. In winter, music moves indoors to the concert halls and the shiny white marble opera house in Bjørvika – an architectural masterpiece as well as a place to hear world-class music played and sung. The city's contemporary music scene has greatly diversified. Young and talented musicians are beginning to receive national and international acclaim. There has been a focus in recent years on the so-called 'Oslo sound', a mix of jazz and electronica. Much of this expansion can be attributed to the spread of clubs, bars and concert venues that enable both the musicians to express themselves and the public to hear them.

Oslo boasts memorable architecture. Twentieth-century additions such as the Rådhuset (The City Hall) find a comfortable place alongside the neoclassical lines of the Royal Palace. Elsewhere here you'll find chunks of living history and architecture combined in places like the old quarter in Gamlebyen, filled with centuries-old houses, well preserved and still occupied. It's a city crammed with works from both the past and the present, while leaving plenty of room for tomorrow's additions.

One tip: if you want to catch a glimpse of people wearing the *bunad*, or national costume, try to time your visit to coincide with a traditional festival such as Constitution Day on 17 May. On this day, Karl Johans street is packed with Norwegians proudly sporting their *bunads*. Otherwise, you'll have to content yourself with viewing them in one of Oslo's historical museums.

⏵ *Tall ships docked in Oslo's harbour*

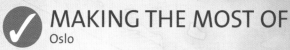

MAKING THE MOST OF
Oslo

Shopping

Oslo can satisfy most shopaholics, with department stores, small boutiques and shops, antique emporiums, flea markets, open markets and countless handicraft and souvenir shops. Most are open 09.00–17.00 Monday to Friday and until 15.00 on Saturday. Department stores have longer hours, staying open until 19.00 or later on weekdays and 18.00 on Saturdays. Only during the holiday season will you find stores open on Sundays.

Traditional Norwegian souvenir shopping would have to include some knitwear, such as a hand-knitted *lusekofte* sweater, brightly coloured mittens, gloves or a scarf. Knitting is a time-honoured tradition in Norway and at school both boys and girls are taught it. You might want to take a tip from Queen Sonja and present your friends with Norwegian pewter pieces – beer mugs, dishes and bowls are frequently decorated with traditional designs. For the child on your list you'll find lots of small cuddly items such as stuffed polar bears, furry seals and even some Norwegian trolls.

If you like your shopping compact, start in the city centre area near Karl Johans Gate. This pedestrian precinct is filled with familiar chain stores such as Benetton and H&M. If you prefer one-stop shopping in a department store or mall, the city centre area is home to Steen & Strøm, Paleet, Glassmagasinet and Byporten. Grünerløkka (see page 84) is a young and hip area. Here, small independent stores are filled with clothes, pottery, handicrafts and even some used book and record shops. Young Norwegian designers frequently launch their products in the shops here.

In Majorstua (see page 100) the streets of Bogstadveien and Hegdehaugsveien are a divine mix of both exclusive and mid-price stores. You could spend an entire day exploring just two streets.

USEFUL SHOPPING PHRASES

What time do the shops open/close?
Når åpner/stenger butikkene?
Nor orpn-er/stehng-er butt-ick-ehne?

How much is it?
Hvor mye koster det?
Vor mew-yer koster deh?

I'd like to buy ...
Jeg kan få ...
Yeh kern for ...

Bygdøy Allé in Frogner (see page 100) is home to a good selection of modern interior design shops. Grønland (see page 84), like Grünerløkka, almost defies description. The markets here are filled with vegetables and ethnic foods and the shops carry everything from fabrics to gold. Take some time to wander the streets of Grønlandsleiret and Smalgangen, where you will find many low-priced shops run by immigrants offering products from their home countries.

If you're planning a trip to Bergen, it's worth saving up some spending money. Although relatively small, the city has long been an important centre of trade in Norway and even contains the country's oldest shopping centre. Bergen's individual boutiques offer products you'll have difficulty finding anywhere else in Norway, or indeed the world, including moose-leather clothes and accessories, excellent woollen garments and replica Viking swords.

Eating & drinking

Traditional Norwegian food comes mostly from the sea. *Laks* (salmon), whether grilled, smoked or marinated, is very popular, as is *reker* (boiled shrimp), *sild* (herring) and *torsk* (cod). Boiled potatoes and other vegetables are normally served alongside meat or fish. You can expect to see pickled herring and *brunost* (a sweet brown goat's cheese) on breakfast buffets along with breads and cereals. A favourite Norwegian dessert is *moltebær syltetøy* (cloudberry jam), served warm with ice cream. *Eplekake* (apple cake) with fresh cream is also popular.

By most standards, Norwegian food is rather bland and heavy, although Oslo does have its share of excellent restaurants. For something a little different, you can try a reindeer, moose or whale steak. Vegetarians and vegans, admittedly, will find the city a challenge, as most menus are based on fish and meat.

At the bottom of the food chain are food wagons and street kiosks, where you can get hot dogs, hamburgers and soft drinks. Next up are the *konditoris*, or bakeries, which sell coffee, fresh pastries and sandwiches. Most have a few tables where you can sit and enjoy your food as you watch the street scene. For more substantial meals, try the *kafeterias*, which serve traditional, simple meals at reasonable prices. At the top end are *kafes* and *restaurants*: Oslo has a wide

PRICE CATEGORIES

The following price guide, used throughout the book, indicates the average price per head for a two-course dinner, excluding drinks. Lunch will usually be a little cheaper in each category.

£ up to 200Kr   ££ 200–300Kr   £££ over 300Kr

variety of traditional and international restaurants, but the prices tend to be high.

Tipping is not required, but most people will round up the bill, and even leave a little extra if the service has been good.

On warm summer days, pick up some sandwiches, desserts and drinks at a *konditori* and head for Frogner Park or Vigeland Park for

△ *Oslo is a seafood lover's paradise*

LUTEFISK

The dictionary defines *lutefisk* (pronounced 'lood-e-fisk') as 'stockfish that has been soaked in lye water, skinned, boned and boiled.' Lye is a strong alkaline liquid containing mainly potassium carbonate, obtained by leaching wood ashes with water. *Lutefisk* is normally served with butter, salt and pepper. The finished *lutefisk* usually has the consistency of gelatine and Norwegians traditionally serve it for Christmas. It's an acquired taste, and not for the weak of stomach.

The history of the dish dates back to Viking times and there are many legends surrounding its origin. Most tales involve dried cod that was subsequently caught in a fire. Water was used to put out the fire, and the dried fish was allowed to sit in the slush of the ash and the water. Someone then ate the fish that had been rehydrated with the resulting lye water, and that person apparently liked it. Anyone trying *lutefisk* for the first time has to wonder if that person was insane or just very hungry.

a picnic. If you like seafood, you can buy freshly caught and cooked shrimps directly from the fishermen at the harbour. Enjoy shelling and eating them as you stroll along the harbour and buy a beer to wash them down with at a local café.

The national drink of Norway, if it had one, would be coffee, served strong and black. If you want to dilute yours with cream or add sugar you will have to ask for it. On the alcoholic side, most Norwegians consume a rather watery pilsner beer, or aquavit, a very strong and bitter spirit.

There are three types of drinking establishments in Oslo. The high-class bars with modern designs tend to be frequented by businesspeople. The low-class, or 'brown', bars, dusty wooden establishments, serve the masses. The third class is chain or themed bars, such as Irish pubs, which are aimed mainly at tourists.

USEFUL DINING PHRASES

I would like a table for ... people, please
Et bord til ..., takk
Eht boor til ..., terk

May I see the menu, please?
Kan jeg få menyen, takk?
Kern yeh for men-ew-en, terk?

I am a vegetarian
Jeg er vegetarianer
Yeh ar veh-geh-ter-iahner

Where is the toilet (restroom), please?
Hvor er toalettene, takk?
Voor ar too-er-lehterner, terk?

May I have the bill, please?
Kan jeg få regningen, takk?
Kern yeh for rehg-ning-ehn, terk?

Entertainment & nightlife

Don't be fooled by first impressions. Underneath Oslo's outwardly conservative atmosphere is a healthy nightlife scene. There are countless cafés, bars and nightclubs to choose from and the vibe ranges from the ultra-trendy to the down-to-earth. Nightlife is an active ingredient of each area. From young and hip Grünerløkka to the more upscale Aker Brygge or the art-conscious cafés of Majorstua, you'll find plenty to keep you occupied. Oslo's nightlife is also very well dressed, and Norwegians expect you to be well shod and stylish. Save your grubby attire for the pub back home.

The first thing you'll discover when night falls and you head out on the town is that there is a huge range of places in Oslo in which you might spend your evening – and your money. What's the difference between a café or a bar and a nightclub? In Oslo it can be hard to tell. Many cafés and bars that serve food during the day morph into a nightclub with a DJ playing music around 21.00–22.00 at night. This may also be the time when a cover charge appears. All restaurants, bars and nightclubs in Oslo, and the whole of Norway for that matter, are smoke-free (see page 148), but many have outdoor tables during the summer, and in the winter lots of places provide outdoor heaters to keep their puffing patrons protected from the cold. Most bars and nightclubs are open until about 03.00, at least on Friday and Saturday nights.

If you prefer the sound of a well-played violin over the twang of a guitar, or the tinkle of a triangle over a thumping R'n'B drumbeat, you'll be pleased to know that Oslo has plenty of gentler musical options to offer. The city is home to a wide range of live stages and concert halls. This is, after all, the home country of Ibsen and Grieg and on almost any given night you'll be able to see one of their works being performed. Classical music is very much a part of Oslo's modern nightlife. The city boasts both a fine philharmonic symphony orchestra and opera company. You'll have plenty of opportunities to hear Grieg as well as more contemporary composers such as David Monrad Johansen, Geirr Tveitt, Fartein

🔺 *When the sun sets, Oslo's wide selection of bars and clubs brings the city to life*

WHAT'S ON
The *What's On in Oslo* brochure produced by the tourist office is a good place to find out what is happening where. *Streetwise*, a free publication, is another good source. Both of these are available in English.

Valen and Pauline Hall. If you think there's nothing new in the world of opera, spend a Tuesday or Thursday evening at the **Underwater Pub** (🚇 Dalsbergstien 4 ☎ 22 46 05 26 🌐 www.underwaterpub.no (Norwegian only)), where students from the State School of Opera try out their skills. And, yes, part of the pub truly is under the sea.

Jazz, fusion and modern folk also have their place in Oslo. Norwegian saxophonist Jan Garbarek is a hot property, while the ethereal and haunting music of the Sami people has been experiencing a revival: one musician to listen out for in this genre is Áilo Gaup. You will still find traces of A-Ha, the Norwegian band of the 1980s that experienced a few fleeting moments in the world rock spotlight.

Traditional folk dancing and singing is also enjoying something of a renaissance, and during the summer months there are plenty of festivals showcasing these activities. A century ago, when Norway was struggling to establish a cultural identity to accompany its newly acquired independence, there was a resurgence in traditional dances such as the polka, *reinlender* and mazurka. In 2005, as Norway celebrated its centenary, there was another wave of nationalism that once again brought these traditions to the forefront. Today troupes of *leikarringen* (folk dancers) appear in competitions all over the country.

◆ *Norway's National Theatre*

Sport & relaxation

SPECTATOR SPORTS

Norwegians spend a lot of time outdoors, skiing in the winter and sailing, fishing and hiking in the summer. Most activities for visitors are linked to the outdoors. Tickets to all major sporting events are available at Norwegian post offices, by calling ❶ 815 33 133 or by logging on to Ⓦ www.billettservice.no

Winter sports

Rock carvings 4,000 years old show ancient Norwegians on skis. Fast forward to the 2010 Winter Olympics, and Norway came away with 23 medals while cross-country skier Marit Bjørgen alone won five, including three golds. He also triumphed, as did Norway, at the FIS Nordic World Ski Championships 2011 at Holmenkollen.

All forms of skiing are popular in Norway – cross-country, downhill and ski jumping. Holmenkollen is the natural centre of winter activities in Oslo, being the host of both the World Cup Biathlon in March each year (see page 8), and family activities such as Barnas Holmenkolldag (see page 9) and the Holmenkollen Ski Marathon. The Holmenkollen centre has recently been renovated

⬤ *Cross-country skiing is just one of many popular winter sports*

and now boasts the world's most modern ski jump; check Ⓦ www.skiforeningen.no (Norwegian only) for information on opening times and facilities.

Football

There are some 1,800 football clubs around the country. Oslo hosts the Norway Cup, the world's largest international football tournament for 12–19s, during the first week of August. More than 30,000 players enter the competition. Ⓦ www.norwaycup.no

Horse racing

Øvrevoll race track (Ⓦ www.ovrevoll.no) is just outside Oslo. The horse-racing season runs from April until December. There is also the **Bjerke Trotting track** (Ⓦ www.bjerke.no – Norwegian only), at Trondheimsveien, with racing on Wednesdays and Saturdays.

PARTICIPATION SPORTS
Golf

Golf is popular in Norway, with several good courses in and around Oslo. For the less energetic, there are also several mini-golf courses.

Winter sports

There are thousands of kilometres of ski trails in and around Oslo, as well as many alpine runs. In the summer, try the ski simulator at Holmenkollen. In winter, there's also ice-skating and dog sledding.

Watersports

If you feel a Viking urge, all manner of boats, from yachts to canoes and sea kayaks, are for rent, but note that plundering and pillaging are no longer allowed. For yacht hire, see Ⓦ www.norwayyachtcharter.com

Accommodation

Oslo can hardly be considered a budget location, and likewise its hotels are often considered expensive by visitors. But the city does have options to suit all pockets, and bargains can be had at weekends and during July and August.

HOTELS

Residence Kristinelund ££ This friendly B&B in an atmospheric 19th-century house is located in a posh residential area off Bygdøy Allé. There are 24 airy rooms (with shared bathrooms), some with balconies. ➋ Kristinelundsveien 2 (Bygdøy Peninsula) ➊ 40 00 24 11 ⓦ www.kristinelund.no ⓝ T-bane; tram: 13, 19 to Nationaltheatret

Thon Hotel Munch ££ A basic hotel, reasonably priced and in a central location that's surprisingly quiet. Some rooms are accessible for visitors with mobility problems. ➋ Munchs Gate 5 (Central Oslo) ➊ 23 21 96 00 ⓦ www.thonhotels.no/munch ⓝ T-bane; tram: 11, 12, 13, 17, 18, 19 to Jernbanetorget; tram: 11, 17, 18 to Tinghuset

Best Western Bondeheimen Hotel ££–£££ A traditional hotel that, despite modernisation, has kept its Norwegian country feel. Business facilities and a Norwegian restaurant are also on-site. ➋ Rosenkrantz

PRICE CATEGORIES

Hotel ratings in this book are based on the cost of a double room for one night. Breakfast is usually included.
£ up to 700Kr **££** 700–1,100Kr **£££** over 1,100Kr

Gate 8 (Central Oslo) ☎ 23 21 41 00 🅦 www.bondeheimen.com
🅝 T-bane: Stortinget; tram: 11, 17, 18 to Prof Aschehougs plass

First Hotel Millennium ££–£££ Atmospheric first-class hotel, renovated in 2011, right in the heart of Oslo near the Parliament building, Akershus Castle and Karl Johans Gate. 🅐 Tollbugata 25 (Central Oslo) ☎ 21 02 28 00 🅦 www.firsthotels.com 🅝 Tram: 13, 19 to Wessels plass

Rica Helsfyr Hotel ££–£££ Although not located in an area covered by this guide, this recently refurbished hotel east of the city is near a T-bane stop and is a good choice for those who want to escape the city's hustle and bustle. 🅐 Strømsveien 108 ☎ 23 06 78 78 🅦 www.rica.no 🅝 T-bane: Helsfyr

Rica Victoria Hotel ££–£££ A centrally located hotel, within walking distance of many of Oslo's main tourist attractions and widespread shopping possibilities. Business facilities and Internet access on-site. 🅐 Rosenkrantz Gate 13 (Central Oslo) ☎ 24 14 70 00 🅦 www.rica.no 🅝 T-bane: Stortinget

Scandic Vulkan ££–£££ Just a couple of kilometres north of central Oslo, this ultra-modern hotel by the Akerselva River opened in October 2011. It's handy for the trendy bars of Grünerløkka, but has its own restaurant, bistro and bar if you're too tired after sightseeing. 🅐 Maridalsveien 13A ☎ 21 05 71 00 🅦 www.scandichotels. com 🅝 Tram: 13 to Schous plass

Thon Hotel Europa ££–£££ A casual and informal hotel within easy reach of the city centre. Guests have use of a nearby fitness facility.

ⓐ St Olavs Gate 31 (Central Oslo) ❶ 23 25 63 00 ⓦ www.thonhotels.no/europa ⓝ T-bane: Nationaltheatret; tram: 11, 17, 18 to Tullinløkka

Thon Hotel Stefan ££–£££ A pleasant, if unexciting, modern hotel in a central location. There is free Wi-Fi. ⓐ Rosenkrantz Gate 1 (Central Oslo) ❶ 23 31 55 00 ⓦ www.thonhotels.no/stefan ⓝ T-bane: Stortinget; tram: 11, 17, 18 to Tinghuset

Clarion Collection Hotel Gabelshus £££ A 15-minute walk from the centre in a quiet, upmarket neighbourhood, this well-furnished hotel offers good value for the price, with free parking and morning and evening buffets. ⓐ Gabels Gate 16 (Holmenkollen, Frogner & Majorstua) ❶ 23 27 65 00 ⓦ www.choicehotels.no ⓝ Tram: 13 to Skillebekk

Norlandia Karl Johan Hotel £££ Smartly renovated hotel that has a long tradition of offering comfortable lodgings and boasts a central location, right on Karl Johans Gate. ⓐ Karl Johans Gate 33 (Central Oslo) ❶ 23 16 17 00 ⓦ www.karljohan.no ⓝ T-bane; tram: 13, 19 to Nationaltheatret

Radisson SAS Plaza Hotel £££ The Radisson's soaring dramatic exterior of tinted blue glass with a needle summit belies its intimate and well-decorated rooms. The views from the upper floors are astonishing (it is, after all, Northern Europe's tallest hotel). A fitness centre with sauna and pool is a further draw. ⓐ Sonja Henies plass 3 (Central Oslo) ❶ 22 05 80 00 ⓦ www.radissonblu.com ⓝ T-bane; tram: 11, 12, 13, 17, 18, 19 to Jernbanetorget

Rica Grand Hotel £££ With its landmark mansard roof and copper tower, Oslo's premier hotel has been an integral part of daily life

◗ Oslo's Rica Grand Hotel has a long history of hospitality

since 1874. Henrik Ibsen, Edvard Munch, Dwight Eisenhower and Henry Ford have all stayed here. ⓐ Karl Johans Gate 31 (Central Oslo) ⓣ 23 21 20 00 ⓦ www.grand.no ⓝ T-bane; tram: 13, 19 to Nationaltheatret

Thon Hotel Cecil £££ Located next to the Parliament in the city centre, just a few steps from Rosenkrantz Gate, this hotel has large, well-equipped rooms with Internet access. ⓐ Stortingsgata 8 (Central Oslo) ⓣ 23 31 48 00 ⓦ www.thonhotels.no/cecil ⓝ T-bane; tram: 13, 19 to Nationaltheatret

Thon Hotel Linne £££ A modern business and conference hotel located only 15 minutes by car or bus from downtown Oslo. There's a licensed bar and restaurant, parking is included in the rate, and the airport express bus also stops nearby. ⓐ Statsråd Mathiesens vei 12 ⓣ 23 17 00 00 ⓦ www.thonhotels.no/linne ⓝ Bus: 60 to Linne Hotell

Thon Hotel Opera £££ Within easy reach of Oslo Central Station. The hotel's décor is modern and somewhat spartan, but the facilities are good and include a fitness centre with sauna, a restaurant with views over Oslo Fjord, and a coffee shop. Disabled access. ⓐ Dronning Eufemias Gate 4 (Central Oslo) ⓣ 24 10 30 30 ⓦ www.thonhotels.no/opera ⓝ T-bane; tram: 11, 12, 13, 17, 18, 19 to Jernbanetorget

Thon Hotel Terminus £££ A modern, well-equipped hotel within walking distance of the main railway station. A basic buffet dinner is included in the room rate on weekdays outside peak season. ⓐ Stenersgatena 10 (Central Oslo) ⓣ 22 05 60 00 ⓦ www.

thonhotels.no/terminus ⓝ T-bane; tram: 11, 12, 13, 17, 18, 19 to Jernbanetorget

Thon Hotel Vika Atrium £££ An efficient, business-oriented hotel on the edge of the Aker Brygge area, close to transport, shops and restaurants. A fitness room and sauna are available. ⓐ Munkedamsveien 45 (Central Oslo) ⓣ 22 83 33 00 ⓦ www.thonhotels.no/vikaatrium ⓝ T-bane; tram: 13, 19 to Nationaltheatret

HOSTELS

Anker Hostel £ This place has an international atmosphere and a spit-and-polish approach to cleanliness. Most rooms have at least four beds, and some have six. Facilities include a laundry, a kitchen and a small bar. Note that linen is not included. ⓐ Storgata 55 (Grünerløkka & Grønland) ⓣ 22 99 72 00 ⓦ www.ankerhostel.no ⓝ Tram: 11, 12, 13, 17 to Hausmanns gate

Oslo Hostel Rønningen YMCA £ A cheap option with singles and doubles as well as rooms with up to four beds. It's located outside of the central areas covered by this guide but is close to a tram stop. The hostel only operates during the summer months and fills up quickly, so book well in advance. Breakfast is included; linen isn't. ⓐ Myrerskogveien 54 ⓣ 21 02 36 00 ⓦ www.oslohostel.com ⓝ Tram: 13, 17 to Grefsen St; bus: 56 to Rønningen

THE BEST OF OSLO

If you have only a limited amount of time in Oslo, here are ten experiences you shouldn't miss.

TOP 10 ATTRACTIONS

- **Norwegian Folk Museum** Over 150 buildings make up Europe's largest open-air museum (see page 94).

- **Akershus Slott (Akershus Castle)** This centuries-old fortress is still used for state occasions and contains the Resistance Museum, which gives a startlingly forthright account of the German occupation of Norway (see pages 62 & 74).

- **Kon-Tiki Museum** Thor Heyerdahl mesmerised the world with his balsa-log raft voyages across the Pacific Ocean in 1947. The raft itself is on permanent display along with artefacts from that voyage and the papyrus boat, the *Ra II* (see page 94).

- **Vikingskipshuset (Viking Ship Museum)** The Viking ships on display – the *Gokstad*, *Tune* and *Oseberg*, all dating from 800–900 – are the best preserved in any museum (see page 97).

- **Munch-museet (Munch Museum)** Edvard Munch's work forms the core of the collection, along with the works of many other Norwegian artists (see page 84). Plans for a new museum have been bogged down in controversy.

- **Rådhuset (The City Hall)** The site of the presentation of the Nobel Peace Prize is either a superb or remarkably ugly piece of architecture, depending on your taste. However you see it, it's certainly dramatic (see page 69).

- **Vigeland Park** Located in Frogner Park, this is one of Oslo's most remarkable attractions. The 212 dramatic bronze, granite and iron sculptures by Gustav Vigeland depict his vision of humanity in all its forms (see page 104).

- **Nasjonalgalleriet (National Gallery)** Only a short walk from Karl Johans Gate is one of Norway's largest collections of important pieces of art and design. Be sure to take a stop in The Edvard Munch Hall to see the world-famous *Skrik* (*The Scream*) (see page 73).

- **Aker Brygge** Once an active shipyard, this abandoned industrial area has been transformed into one of Oslo's most attractive waterfront areas, filled with shops and restaurants. It's a perfect place to sip a glass of wine and view the fortress of Akershus across the water (see page 62).

- **Holmenkollen ski jump** The world-famous ski jump was revamped for the 2011 World Ski Championships, and is a must-visit for any keen skier (see page 102).

🔽 *The port of Oslo*

Suggested itineraries

HALF-DAY: OSLO IN A HURRY

If you only have half a day, put on some comfy shoes for a walk
through the centre to take in some of Oslo's top sights. Starting at
the main railway station, Oslo S, walk west along Karl Johans Gate
towards the Royal Palace (Det Kongelige Slott). The first building on
the right is Oslo Domkirke (Cathedral). As you continue along Karl
Johans Gate you will come to Stortinget, the home of the Norwegian
Parliament. Turn left onto Kongens Gate, where you will find the
Norwegian Architecture Museum. Turn left again onto Revierstredet
where you will see Engebret Café, Oslo's oldest eatery. Turn right

● Aker Brygge is the perfect place to spend a sunny day

onto Kirkegata, and you will pass the Museum of Contemporary Art (entrance on Myntgata). At the end of Kirkegata, you will come to a drawbridge which will take you over Kongens Gate and into Akershus Castle. Work your way north through the fortress and exit through a gate onto Akersgate. Turn right onto Rådhusgata to see Christiania Torv (Square) and the Theatre Museum. Retrace your steps and continue west on Rådhusgata until you come to Rådhuset (The City Hall). Walk around Rådhuset, through Fridtjof Nansens plass and onto Roald Amundsens Gate, where you will find the National Theatre. Cross Karl Johans Gate and you will be beside the University. Turn left on Kristian IVs Gate which will take you past the National Art Gallery and the History Museum. At Frederiks Gate you can cross into the gardens of the Royal Palace. Work your way south through the Royal Palace complex until you emerge onto Drammensveien and go west. Passing the Ibsen Museum, turn left onto Huitfeldts Gate and left again onto Cort Adelers Gate. This will take you into Aker Brygge. Find a nice restaurant on the waterfront to enjoy lunch and a cold Norwegian beer – you deserve it.

1 DAY: TIME TO SEE A LITTLE MORE

A whole day gives you time to explore one or two of the sights on the half-day walk in more depth. Alternatively, take a ferry from Rådhusbrugge (City Hall Quay) to Bygdøynes. As you alight you will see the *Gjøa*, the first ship to traverse the Northwest Passage in 1903–6. Just past the *Gjøa* is a large plaza, onto which three major maritime museums face: the Fram Museum, the Kon-Tiki Museum and the Norwegian Maritime Museum. After exploring at least one of these museums, it is worth the extra 1-km (1/2-mile) walk to perhaps the best of them all: follow Bygdøynesveien, turn right onto Langviksveien and left onto Huk Aveny, which will bring you to the entrance of the Viking Ship Museum. From this museum, retrace your steps to Langviksveien. From here, if you still have time, you can continue north to the Norwegian Folk Museum. From the Folk Museum, continue north on Langviksveien, turn right on Museumsveien, and left onto Huk Aveny. At the end of Huk Aveny, you can catch a ferry back to the waterfront and enjoy a beer.

2–3 DAYS: TIME TO SEE MUCH MORE

The half-day and one-day sightseeing walks can easily be expanded into two or three days if some of the museums take your fancy. But if not, there's still plenty more to pack in. Other sights worth visiting include the Munch Museum, the Holmenkollen ski jump, Vigeland Park and Museum, and Gamlebyen. Oslo also has many smaller museums dedicated to just about anything you can imagine. Spend at least one evening wining and dining with the locals in Grünerløkka.

LONGER: ENJOYING OSLO TO THE FULL

If you have lots of time, you can easily spend several more days taking in what Oslo has to offer. If you feel a need to get away from the city, however, you can discover Norway outside Oslo. Perhaps the best way is to take the 'Norway in a Nutshell' tour (see page 118). It can be done in two days (Oslo to Bergen), but you may want to spend up to a week to really get a feel for the country, by adding loops to Stavanger and Sognefjord. Other options include one- or two-day trips down the east coast of Oslofjorden to Drøbak, Fredrikstad and Halden – by car, bus, train or ferry – or a two- or three-day excursion north to Lillehammer, Røros and Trondheim. Perhaps the best of all for a truly get-away-from-it-all feeling is the coastal cruise north from Bergen. You can go as far north as time and funds allow.

○ *A gentle excursion on Oslofjorden*

Something for nothing

Although Oslo isn't considered the most expensive city in the world, it is in the global top twenty. The cost of living here is definitely on the high side – as is the case in many Scandinavian countries. Even visitors with deep pockets and a wallet full of credit cards will be pleased, after a few days, if they can seek out something to do in Oslo which is either free or cheap. Luckily, there is a whole host of possibilities on offer depending on the weather, ranging from museums to parks to winter sports.

In summer, you can't go wrong with a trip to the park. Vigeland Park (see page 104) is Norway's most visited attraction, and is filled with more than 200 sculptures by noted artist Gustav Vigeland. The same artist also designed the clever layout of the park: set off exploring the paths and admiring the sculptures, and you'll be entertained for a couple of hours or more. Another great option for a relaxing day out is a trip to the **Botanical Gardens** (ⓐ Sars Gate 1 ⓘ 22 85 50 50 ⓦ www.nhm.uio.no ⓛ 07.00–21.00 Mon–Fri, 10.00–21.00 Sat & Sun (mid-Mar–Sept); 07.00–17.00 Mon–Fri, 10.00–17.00 Sat & Sun (Oct–mid-Mar) ⓝ T-bane: Tøyen; bus: 31; tram: 17 to Lakkegata skole), which house a beautiful collection of Norwegian and foreign plants.

Winter is a different kettle of fish, offering some rather more adrenalin-pumping, if colder, outdoor activities. When snow is lying on the ground, take the bus out to **Akebakken Luge** (ⓐ Akebakken, 8 km (5 miles) from the city centre ⓝ Bus: 56 to Akebakken) to watch – or join in with – the thrill-seekers sledding down this popular luge track. Alternatively, it's free to skate on one of the many outdoor ice rinks which appear around Oslo during the winter months; the only small cost involved is for skate rental. Most rinks are open every day from December to March.

Those who love cultural attractions more than outdoor activities can also find free or cheap things to do. The Astrup Fearnley Museum of Modern Art (see page 71) is home to an extensive collection of post-war art from Norwegian and international artists. For an historical overview of the city, you can't go wrong with a visit to the Oslo City Museum (see page 105), which is set in the distinguished Frogner Manor. Here, the house and grounds alone would make the trip worthwhile; entry to the museum, which sets out Oslo's history using models, photographs, objects and paintings, is also free. The museum offers historical town walks – call in advance to arrange. A deeper insight into Norway's military history is provided by the Forsvarsmuseet (Norwegian Armed Forces Museum, see page 71), which spans the whole period from the Vikings to the 1950s and uses a combination of dioramas, models and historical objects to re-create this fascinating segment of history.

🔺 *Gustav Vigeland's sculpture park is an unforgettable sight*

When it rains

It's raining? Throw on your best cape and deerstalker hat and head to Æreslunden, Oslo Cathedral's Memorial Graveyard, and contemplate the loss of such notable figures as Edvard Munch and Henrik Ibsen. If you don't want to get wet, then Oslo has a vast range of museums for every taste that will absorb your time. When it's pouring down outside, visit the Kon-Tiki Museum (see page 94) and imagine how the sailors must have felt on board Thor Heyerdahl's balsa-log raft during his legendary crossing of the Pacific Ocean in 1947. Going back even further, original Viking ships are on display in the Viking Ship Museum (see page 97). If art and culture are more your thing, head for the National Gallery (see page 73) or the Munch Museum (see page 84) – both are world-class art museums whose exhibits will occupy you until the rain dies down.

Bærums Verk is a delightful collection of buildings from 1610 that are filled with craft shops and restaurants (see page 100). You may have to dodge the raindrops between the buildings but it's a good way to spend a few hours on a dreary day sipping hot chocolate and admiring the work of artisans. It takes on a festive air at Christmas (see page 12).

When only a mall crawl will satisfy your need to be active but remain dry, head to the Byporten centre (see page 77), next to Central Station, or Steen & Strøm, also in the city centre, an inspired collection of shops offering everything from clothes and books to perfumes, furniture, shoes and toys.

⬥ *A visit to the National Gallery is a fine solution for a rainy day*

On arrival

TIME DIFFERENCE

Oslo's clocks follow Central European Time (CET). During Daylight Saving Time (end Mar–end Oct), the clocks go forward one hour.

ARRIVING

By air

Oslo International Airport is located at Gardermoen, about 50 km (30 miles) north of the city. It has facilities including banks, ATMs, currency exchange, restaurants, tourist information desks, newsagents, gift shops and a pharmacy. The airport is usually busy (an expansion is planned, to be completed in 2017), and the layout requires some long walks, so allow extra time on arriving or departing. If you haven't acquired any Norwegian kroner (Kr) before leaving your home country, make sure you get some at the airport, as few local businesses accept foreign currencies.

From the airport, high-speed trains (Flytoget) go to Oslo S, the city's central railway station. The trains run every ten minutes, and take about 20 minutes to get there. The fare is 170Kr. There are also express buses to Oslo S operated by SAS Transport Service. The buses leave every 20–30 minutes, and travel time is about 40 minutes. The fare is 140Kr one way or 240Kr return. Taxis are available outside the arrivals area, but the fare to central Oslo is expensive, starting at 695Kr. There are desks for all major car rental companies at the airport.

Oslo is served by most international airlines. Domestic flights to other parts of Norway also leave from Gardermoen.

Flytoget ⓦ www.flytoget.no

Oslo International Airport ❶ 91 50 64 00 ⓦ www.osl.no

SAS Transport Service buses ⓦ www.flybussen.no/oslo

IF YOU GET LOST, TRY …

Excuse me, do you speak English?
Unnskyld meg, snakker du engelsk?
Unshewl mey, snerkur doo ehng-erlsk?

How do I get to ...?
Hvordan kommer jeg til ...?
Voordern kommer yeh til ...?

Can you show me on my map?
Kan du vise meg på kartet?
Kern doo veesur meh po kertur?

Sandefjord Airport Torp (⦿ www.torp.no) is located 110 km (70 miles) southwest of Oslo, and is Norway's second-largest international airport. Several low-cost airlines are now using this airport as a second gateway to Oslo. The **Torp Express bus service** (☎ 67 98 04 80 ⦿ www.torpekspressen.no) connects with some flights and takes about two hours to get to the main bus station in Oslo – however, it is not available for all flights so do check in advance. Alternatively, catch a local bus or take a taxi to Sandefjord railway station, then a train to Oslo. If you have hired a car (all major rental agencies have offices here too), simply follow Highway E18 all the way to the city.

Rygge International Airport (⦿ www.en.ryg.no), south of the city, is the destination for Ryanair flights from Newcastle, Manchester, Liverpool, London Gatwick and London Stansted. Travellers will find a

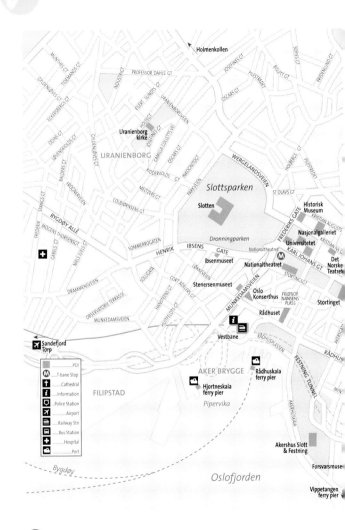

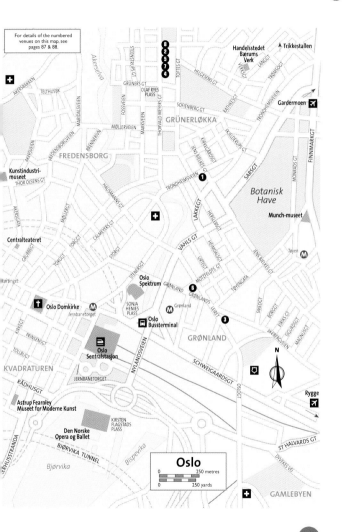

For details of the numbered
venues on this map, see
pages 87 & 88.

free shuttle bus to the station connecting with flight arrivals. Trains take a little under an hour to get to Oslo, while the express bus to the city takes an hour.

By rail

Oslo Sentralstasjon (Central Station ⓐ Jernbanetorget 1 ⓦ www.nsb.no ⓛ 06.00–23.15 Mon–Fri, 10.00–18.00 Sat, 10.00–23.15 Sun) is simply called Oslo S, and is located at the eastern end of Karl Johans Gate near the city centre. Oslo S is the main transportation link in the city. Trains from continental Europe, from other parts of Scandinavia and from other cities in Norway all arrive here, as do the buses and trains from the airports. The main bus station is adjacent to Oslo S and can be reached by an overhead walkway.

Oslo S has many facilities, including an InterRail centre with showers, plus an efficient Tourist Information Centre that can provide maps, information, and assist with currency exchange, hotel reservations and also sell you an Oslo Card. There is also a post office, an Internet café, restaurants and bars inside the station. Taxis, buses and trams are just outside the station. There is also an underground (T-bane) station.

The adjacent shopping centre, Byporten, can be accessed directly from the main gallery. On the southern side is Østbanehallen, the old part of the station, which has been converted into a small shopping arcade.

By road

Oslo Bussterminal (ⓐ Schweigaardsgate 10), the main bus station, is situated on the north side of Oslo's central railway station, which makes transfers between the two very easy. All local bus services, as well as those from further afield, arrive and depart from here.

Cars must pay a 26Kr toll each time they enter Oslo. The city has many one-way streets, which can make driving around confusing, although traffic congestion is not a problem. Parking in Oslo is expensive and regulations are strict. In parts of the centre it can cost up to 66Kr for a maximum of two hours, although with a VisitOslo pass parking is free in municipal parking spaces up to a maximum of 24 hours. The Oslo municipal website Ⓦ www.oslo.kommune.no has more information, as does Ⓦ www.visitoslo.com/en/transport/by-car. Alternatively, leave your car at your hotel or in a privately run car park, which costs about 300Kr a day.

By water

International ferries arrive and depart from two piers. Vippetangen pier is just below Akershus Castle, and Hjortneskaia pier is adjacent to Aker Brygge. Both are on the waterfront close to the centre of Oslo. Ferries to islands in the Oslo fjord leave from Vippetangen. Ferries to the Bygdøy Peninsula leave from Rådhuskaia pier, in front of Rådhuset (The City Hall). These ferries only run in the warmer months – around May until the end of September.

TRAFIKANTEN

Trafikanten is an information office for public transportation in and around Oslo. It is located next to Oslo S, with other offices at Aker Brygge and Gardermoen airport. The office has timetables for trains, buses, trams, the underground (T-bane) and ferries that operate in Oslo, the greater Oslo area and Central Eastern Norway. ⓐ Jernbanetorget 1 ⓣ 81 50 01 76 Ⓦ www.trafikanten.no Ⓛ 07.00–20.00 Mon–Fri, 08.00–18.00 Sat & Sun

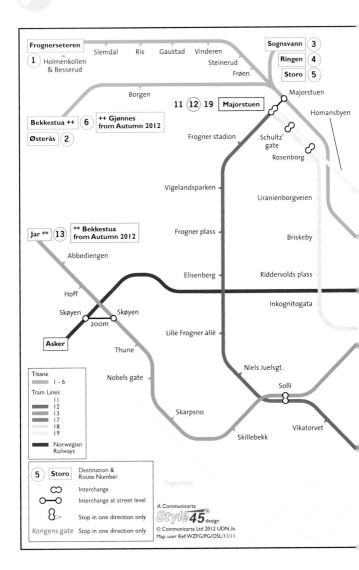

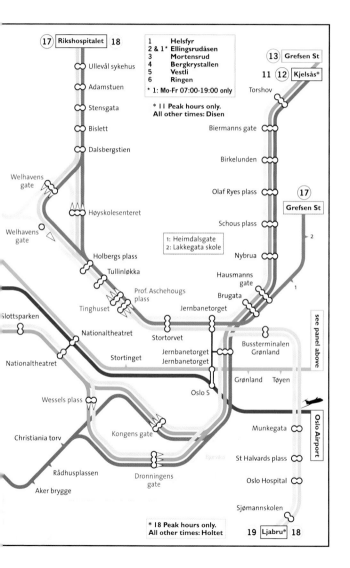

1	Helsfyr
2 & 1*	Ellingsrudåsen
3	Mortensrud
4	Bergkrystallen
5	Vestli
6	Ringen

* 1: Mo-Fr 07:00-19:00 only

* 11 Peak hours only.
All other times: Disen

1: Heimdalsgate
2: Lakkegata skole

* 18 Peak hours only.
All other times: Holtet

FINDING YOUR FEET

Finding your feet in Oslo is easy. This is a user-friendly city, and the people are open and generous. Many attractions and hotels are close enough to the centre that they can be reached on foot, and efficient public transport gives access to those that can't. Crime is not a worry if you take the normal precautions. However, prices and taxes are high, so be prepared to pay for everything from road tolls to toilets. Be warned that many attractions close on a Monday – this might be a good time to head out of the city or to the shops.

Note that the suffix 'et' in Norwegian means 'the'. When you see signs for 'Rådhuset', 'Nationaltheatret' or 'Slottet', for example, this simply means 'the City Hall', 'the National Theatre' or 'the Palace'.

OSLO PASS

If you intend to visit a number of attractions in a short period of time, you should invest in the Oslo Pass. It gives free admission to most museums and attractions, free travel on public transport (except night buses), free parking in municipal car parks, and discounts on sightseeing and car rental and at restaurants and amusement parks. The card is available for periods of 24, 48 or 72 hours; there are no family passes, but a child's pass is available at a discounted rate. It is sold at Tourist Information Centres, most major hotels, some Narvesen kiosks, at Trafikanten (see page 55), or online at ⓦ www.visitoslo.com. An information booklet outlining all the benefits comes with the Oslo Pass.

An Oslo Package is also available, which includes hotel accommodation as well as the Oslo Pass.

ORIENTATION

Karl Johans Gate is the main street in central Oslo. It runs east–west, with Oslo S at the eastern end and the Royal Palace at the western end. Most hotels, as well as many of the city's attractions, are within a 15-minute walk of Karl Johans Gate. The waterfront, Aker Brygge, Rådhuset and Akershus Castle are just a few blocks south of Karl Johans Gate. Most streets, especially those in central Oslo, follow a standard grid pattern.

GETTING AROUND

Getting around the city is no problem. The centre part of the city is easily and safely walkable, and considering the Norwegians' penchant for hiking, this is the preferred mode of transport. If you want to travel a little further afield, the public transport system, consisting of buses, trams and T-bane (metro, subway), is very efficient. Tickets for single trips cost 28Kr in advance, or 44Kr if purchased from the driver of a bus or tram, and are valid on all forms of transport. Advance tickets can be purchased from 7-Eleven stores, Narvesen or Mix kiosks, and from Trafikanten (see page 55). Daily passes cost 75Kr. Multi-day passes are also available. The Oslo Pass gives free transport during the daytime and evening, but not late at night. Note that there is an honour system regarding tickets, and the fine for travelling without a ticket is a hefty 750Kr.

Taxis are easy to find and use in Oslo. They are safe and clean, but can be expensive. The fare starts at around 60Kr plus up to 21Kr per kilometre ($^{1}/_{2}$ mile) during the day. In the evening and at weekends and holidays, fares are considerably more expensive. It's cheaper to flag a taxi rather than to call one, as the meter starts running when a called cab is dispatched and you can owe a small fortune before the taxi even picks you up.

Car hire

Rental cars are readily available, and most major rental agencies are represented at both the airport and in Oslo. However, rental car rates are very high, and car insurance is extra. Some local rental agencies offer lower rates, but the cars can be questionable, and they have been known to charge for 'extras'. If you get a traffic ticket, the fine will be automatically charged to the credit card you used to hire the car. Major rental agencies include:

Avis Ⓦ www.avis.no (Norwegian only)
Gardermoen Airport ❶ 67 25 55 10
Sandefjord Airport Torp ❶ 33 46 95 50
City ❷ Munkedamsveien 27 ❶ 23 23 92 02
Budget Ⓦ www.budget.no (Norwegian only)
Gardermoen Airport ❶ 67 25 55 20
Sandefjord Airport Torp ❶ 33 46 60 50
City ❷ Munkedamsveien 27 ❶ 22 01 76 10
Europcar Ⓦ www.europcar.no
Gardermoen Airport ❶ 64 81 05 60
Sandefjord Airport Torp ❶ 33 44 63 70
City ❷ Munkedamsveien at Dronning Mauds Gate 10–11 ❶ 22 83 12 42
Hertz Ⓦ www.hertz.no
Gardermoen Airport ❶ 64 81 05 50
Sandefjord Airport Torp ❶ 33 47 15 38
Oslo S ❷ Jernbanetorget 1 ❶ 22 21 00 00
Rent-a-Wreck Ⓦ www.rent-a-wreck.no
Gardermoen Airport ❶ 63 92 65 90
Sixt Ⓦ www.sixt.com
Sandefjord Airport Torp ❶ 33 47 68 00

---

❶ *Urban life plus fjords and mountains make for an interesting visit*

# THE CITY OF
Oslo

Central Oslo

The centre of Oslo is a hive of activity, and a focal point for locals, young and old. Karl Johans Gate and the surrounding area is where you will find the greatest concentration of shops, restaurants, bars and music venues, in particular concert and opera halls. If you're more in the mood for clubs and discos, head to Rosenkrantz Gate, and for blues and jazz clubs try Stortovet.

SIGHTS & ATTRACTIONS

Aker Brygge
Once an active shipyard, this large chunk of Oslo's downtown waterfront has now been transformed into a trendy shopping and entertainment district not unlike San Francisco's Fisherman's Wharf. It's a great place to enjoy a glass of wine or a fancy dinner while taking in a panoramic view of the Akershus Castle across the water. The restaurants tend to be at the pricey end of the scale – but it won't cost you a krone to wander the waterfront.
③ Stranden ① 22 83 26 80 ⓦ www.akerbrygge.no ⓝ T-bane: Nationaltheatret; tram: 12 to Aker Brygge

Akershus Slott & Festning (Akershus Castle & Fortress)
This is probably the most striking sight in Oslo. King Haakon V ordered the construction of the fortress to protect the city after he declared Oslo the capital of Norway in 1299. Over the centuries the structure has been subject to attacks, fires, expansions, improvements and renovations. It is still under the control of the military, and as such may be closed at any time for military or state functions.

◆ *Aker Brygge still retains remnants of its heritage*

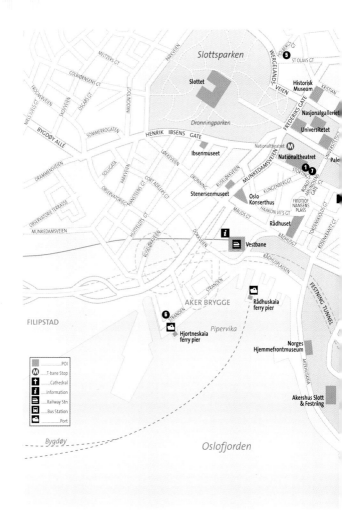

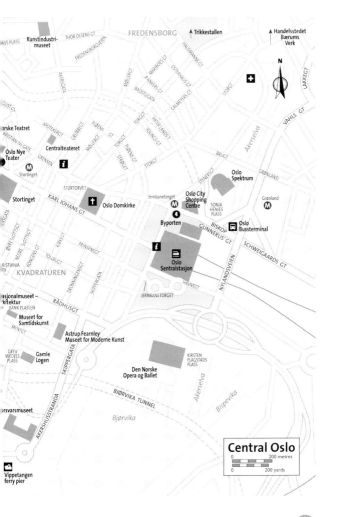

Central Oslo

0   200 metres
0   200 yards

KARL JOHAN

The famous former King of Sweden (and Norway), Karl Johan, is better known to the rest of the world as Jean Bernadotte. Born of humble origins in rural France, he rose to power as one of Napoleon's marshals – and the Emperor's brother-in-law. When he was offered the crown of Sweden after the disastrous French retreat from Moscow he promptly accepted it and then led the Swedish army against his former master. A born survivor, he was the only member of Napoleon's court to establish a royal dynasty.

The fortress is strategically located on the eastern shore of the harbour, with perfect vantage points. Gun towers were added in 1559, and for the next 200 years it was further fortified with moats and ramparts. From 1637 to 1648 it was developed into a Renaissance royal residence, and most of the luxurious state rooms, mausoleums and chapels date from this time. The tombs of Kings Haakon VII and Olaf V lie beneath the main chapel. By the early 19th century the requirement for defence was relaxed, and many of the ramparts were removed to make room for public space.

Akershus became infamous during World War II, when the Nazis took control of Norway and used it as a headquarters and as a site to execute many Norwegian patriots. The Resistance Museum, which is part of the complex, graphically describes the German occupation and the Norwegian resistance movement (see page 74).

Today Akershus is one of Oslo's top tourist attractions. Aside from the lavish state rooms and chapels, the dungeons are also worth a look. There is an information centre just inside Sortieporten, and guided tours are available. The changing of the guard takes place every day at 13.30. 🅰 Akersgata ☎ 23 09 35 53 🕐 10.00–16.00 Mon–Sat, 12.30–16.00 Sun (May–Aug); 12.00–17.00 Sat–Sun, closed Mon–Fri (Sept–Apr) Ⓝ Tram: 12 to Christiania Torv ❶ Admission charge

Christiania Torv

This was Oslo's original market square, renamed with the old city name in 1958. In the 1990s the area was made vehicle-free when a tunnel was created to divert traffic. Now it's a very pleasant area, surrounded by historic buildings and filled with outdoor cafés. Markets are still occasionally held here. 🅰 Kvadraturen Ⓝ Tram: 12 to Christiania Torv

Karl Johans Gate

Located in the heart of Oslo, Karl Johans Gate is the best known and liveliest thoroughfare in the city, if not the entire country. Named after King Karl Johan, the street was designed by architect H D F Linstow in 1840 and is home to many of Norway's top institutions, such as Slottet (The Royal Palace), Stortinget (The Norwegian Parliament) and Nationaltheatret (The National Theatre). Lined with shops, restaurants and cafés, Karl Johan is great for shopping and eating. In winter the upper part of the street is transformed into a skating rink.

Oslo Domkirke (Cathedral)

This beautifully ornate building dating from 1699 is the principal church for the diocese of Oslo. Over the years it has undergone many renovations and the various architectural styles are reflected in the decorative aspects. Among some of the prominent adornments are a stained-glass window by artist Emmanuel Vigeland (brother of

◆ *Not everyone liked the City Hall's stark, modern lines when it was built*

sculptor Gustav Vigeland), a silver sculpture of the Last Supper by
Arrigo Minerbi and bronze doors by Dagfin Werenskiold. The
marvellous painted ceiling was created by Hugo Louis Mohr
between 1936 and 1950. The church has played and continues to
play a prominent role in the city: in 2001 the wedding of Crown
Prince Haakon and Crown Princess Mette-Marit was held here.
The cathedral reopened in 2010 after four years of renovation.

ⓐ Stortorvet ① 23 62 90 10 ⓦ www.oslodomkirke.no Ⓝ Tram: 11, 17, 18 to Stortorvet

Rådhuset (The City Hall)

Oslo's City Hall is best known as the location from which the Nobel Peace Prize is awarded each year in December. Designed by Arnstein Arneberg and Magnus Poulsson and opened in 1950, it is a splendid example of modernist architecture, although it was a long time before residents warmed to such a radical departure from the norm. The ceremonial main hall of the complex covers 1,519 sq m (16,350 sq ft) of space and is graced by Henrik Sørenson's oil painting, the largest in Europe, on the rear wall. ⓐ Fridtjof Nansens plass ① 23 46 12 00 ⓛ 09.00–18.00 daily Ⓝ Tram: 12 to Rådhusplassen

Slottet – Det Kongelige Slott (The Royal Palace)

This imposing royal residence dominates the west end of Karl Johans Gate. It was commissioned by King Karl Johan of Sweden following his ascent to the throne in 1818, after Norway had been ceded to Sweden by Denmark. The king was keen to emphasise his claim on Norway, and commissioning this palace was an important aspect of his PR campaign. Work on the elaborate neoclassical structure began in 1825 but it overran its schedule and budget; it was not completed until 1848, by which time the king had died. In fact, the palace was seldom used by the Swedish monarchs and often shut up in darkness; when the first king of Norway, Haakon, took over the palace in 1905 it was considered uninhabitable, with no running water or toilets, and Haakon was reluctant to burden the state with the expense of renovation. It was only in 1991, on King Harald's accession, that a full evaluation was carried out and the decay declared to be even worse than had been feared; the restoration costs are still controversial and work has only been partly carried out. However, some state rooms have been fully (and magnificently) renovated and are open to the public.

Tours of the interior are restricted, but normally available in summer: call for more information. The gardens surrounding the palace are always open to the public. There is a changing of the guard every day at 13.30. ❷ Henrik Ibsens Gate 1 ❶ 81 53 31 33 ❿ www.kongehuset.no ❻ Tours in English: 12.00, 14.00, 14.20 Mon–Thur & Sat, 14.00, 14.20, 16.00 Fri & Sun (late June–mid-Aug only) ❶ Book tours in advance, admission charge

Stortinget (The Norwegian Parliament)
Norway's National Assembly building was built in the 1860s of yellow brick and reddish granite. The assembly chamber, which seats the 169 Members of Parliament, was designed to resemble an amphitheatre. The building has been richly embellished, both inside and out, by various Norwegian artists; look out for the tapestry, *Solens Gang*, by artist Karen Holtsmark. Guided tours can be booked in advance. ❷ Karl Johans Gate 22 ❶ 23 31 31 80 ❿ www.stortinget.no (Norwegian only) ❻ Office: 10.00–15.00 Mon–Fri (mid-Aug–mid-Dec only); tour times vary ❿ T-bane: Stortinget

Universitetet (The University)
The University of Oslo dominates one side of Karl Johans Gate. The three buildings of the complex are in the neoclassical style and together with the National Theatre create an imposing atmosphere. The Aula, an auditorium dating from 1911, houses several murals by Edvard Munch (he considered them to be his masterpiece). Until Rådhuset was built, the Nobel Peace Prize was presented in the Aula. ❷ Karl Johans Gate ❶ 22 85 50 50 ❿ www.uio.no ❿ T-bane; tram: 13, 19 to Nationaltheatret

CULTURE

Astrup Fearnley Museet for Moderne Kunst (Astrup Fearnley Museum of Modern Art)

Home to an extensive collection of post-war art from a large number of Norwegian and international artists, this privately owned museum opened in 1993. In September 2012 the museum plans to move into two new Renzo Piano-designed buildings in Tjuvholmene. 🅐 Dronningensgate 4 🆃 22 93 60 60 🆆 www.afmuseet.no 🅛 12.00–17.00 Wed–Sun, closed Mon & Tues 🅝 Tram: 12, 13, 19 to Dronningensgate

Forsvarsmuseet (Norwegian Armed Forces Museum)

Another part of the Akershus complex is devoted to Norway's military history from the Vikings to the 1950s. Highlights include the unions with Denmark and Sweden, the German invasion and the Battle of the Atlantic during World War II. The museum incorporates dioramas, models and historical objects to re-create this fascinating segment of history. 🅐 Neder Akershus Festning 🆃 23 09 35 82 🆆 www.forsvaret.no 🅛 10.00–17.00 Mon–Fri, 11.00–17.00 Sat & Sun (May–Aug); 10.00–16.00 Tues–Fri, 11.00–17.00 Sat & Sun, closed on Mon (Sept–Apr) 🅝 Tram: 12 to Christiania Torv

Gamle Logen

This building has had many uses since its inauguration in 1839. It was here that Vidkun Quisling was sentenced to death for treason at the end of World War II. At various times in the intervening years the building has served as a place for city council meetings, a concert hall and labour office. Finally, in 1980, the Oslo Summer Opera moved in and now the building is once again being used for musical events.

@ Grev Wedels Plass 2 ❶ 22 33 44 70 Ⓦ www.logen.no Ⓝ Tram: 12 to Christiania Torv

Historisk Museum

The Historical Museum actually comprises the four university museums, Oldsaksamlingen (National Antiquities Collection), Etnografisk Samling (Ethnographic Museum), Antikksamlingen (Classical Antiques Collection) and Myntkabinettet (Collection of Coins & Medals). Together they thoroughly document Norwegian history from the earliest settlements to the present day. @ Frederiks Gate 2 ❶ 22 85 99 00 Ⓦ www.khm.uio.no ❶ 10.00–17.00 Tues–Sun, closed Mon (mid-May–mid-Sept); 11.00–16.00 Tues–Sun, closed Mon (mid-Sept–mid-May) Ⓝ T-bane: Nationaltheatret; tram: 11, 17, 18 to Tullinløkka

Ibsenmuseet

The Ibsen Museum, once home of Norway's most celebrated playwright, has been lovingly and painstakingly restored to the decoration and furnishings of his period. Ibsen and his wife lived here from 1895 until his death in 1906. Guided tours of Ibsen's apartment are given on the hour. @ Henrik Ibsens Gate 26 ❶ 22 12 35 50 Ⓦ www.ibsenmuseet.no ❶ 11.00–18.00 daily (mid-May–mid-Sept); 11.00–16.00 Mon–Wed, Fri–Sun, 11.00–18.00 Thur (mid-Sept–mid-May) Ⓝ T-bane; tram: 13, 19 to Slottsparken
❶ Admission charge

Museet for Samtidskunst (Museum of Contemporary Art)

This museum, housed in an Art Nouveau building, contains Norway's largest collection of Norwegian and international post-war art. The permanent collection is so big that only part of it is on display at any one time. Famous works include Gunnar Gundersen's *Winter Sun* and Per Manning's photographic portraits of animals. ⓐ Bankplassen 4 ⓘ 21 98 20 00 ⓦ www.nationalmuseum.no ⓛ 11.00–17.00 Tues, Wed & Fri, 11.00–19.00 Thur, 12.00–17.00 Sat & Sun, closed Mon ⓝ T-bane: Stortinget; bus: 60 to Bankplassen; tram: 12 to Christiania Torv

Nasjonalgalleriet (National Gallery)

Norway's National Gallery is home to the country's largest public collection of paintings, sculptures, drawings, engravings and other art forms. The Edvard Munch Hall contains a number of the artist's most famous works, including one of only two painted versions of *Skrik* (*The Scream*) available to the public. The museum also features the work of other Norwegian artists and foreign masters, including Christian Krohg, El Greco, Modigliani, Peter Blake and Harald Sohlberg. ⓐ Universitetsgata 13 ⓘ 21 98 20 00 ⓦ www.national museum.no ⓛ 10.00–18.00 Tues–Wed & Fri, 10.00–19.00 Thur, 11.00–17.00 Sat & Sun, closed Mon ⓝ T-bane: Nationaltheatret; tram: 11, 17, 18 to Tullinløkka

Nasjonalmuseet – arkitektur (National Museum of Architecture)

It is fitting that the national architecture museum should be located in the former Bank of Norway, an important part of Norwegian architectural history in itself, dating back to 1830. The building was renovated in 2008 by a renowned Norwegian architect, Sverre Fehn. There is a separate exhibition pavilion in the garden. ⓐ Bankplassen 3 ⓘ 21 98 20 00 ⓦ www.national museum.no ⓛ 11.00–17.00 Tues, Wed & Fri, 11.00–19.00 Thur, 12.00–17.00 Sat & Sun, closed Mon ⓝ T-bane: Stortinget; bus: 60 to Bankplassen

Nationaltheatret (The National Theatre)

Oslo's National Theatre opened its doors in 1899 with a production of Ibsen's *An Enemy of the People* and it has consistently kept the playwright's work at the core of its repertoire ever since. You'll get more than just a night at the theatre here: it houses one of the country's finest art collections, with works by Vigeland, Werenskiold, Fjell and Krohg. The Baroque-style building itself is also noteworthy: it was designed by Henrik Bull and is typical of late 19th-century European theatre architecture. ❸ Johanne Dybwads plass 1, off Stortingsgata ❶ Information: 22 00 14 00; tickets: 81 50 08 11 ⓦ www.nationaltheatret.no (Norwegian only) Ⓝ T-bane; tram: 13, 19 to Nationaltheatret

Norges Hjemmefrontmuseum (Norwegian Resistance Museum)

Housed in one of the old buildings of the Akershus Castle complex, near the memorial on the spot where Norwegian patriots were executed by the Germans in World War II, this museum was created through the initiative of people who had been actively engaged in the Norwegian Resistance. Five years of occupation from invasion to liberation are uncompromisingly re-created through documents, newspapers, posters, artefacts and sound recordings. ❸ Building 21, Akershus Festning ❶ 23 09 31 38 ⓦ http://mil.no ⏱ 10.00–17.00 Mon–Sat, 11.00–17.00 Sun (June–Aug); 10.00–16.00 Mon–Fri, 11.00–16.00 Sat & Sun (Sept–May)

Den Norske Opera og Ballet (The Norwegian National Opera & Ballet)

The new opera house in Bjørvika is a landmark in Oslo, and definitely worth a visit. If possible, get tickets for a performance; if not, at least take a guided tour to see the spectacular modern architecture close up. Traditional operas and ballets are performed here, along

⬥ *Visit the National Theatre to see Ibsen's famous plays*

with more experimental concerts. ❸ Kirsten Flagstads Plass 1
🎫 Information: 21 42 21 00; box office: 21 42 21 21 🌐 www.operaen.no
🚇 T-bane; tram: 11, 12, 13, 17, 18, 19 to Jernbanetorget

Det Norske Teatret (Theatre of Norway)

The company was founded in 1913 but didn't have a permanent
home until 1985, when the curtain went up on this ultra-modern
construction. It is the main venue in Oslo for works in Norwegian,

both classical and modern. Ⓐ Kristian IVs Gate 8 Ⓣ 22 42 43 44
Ⓦ www.detnorsketeatret.no (Norwegian only) Ⓝ Tram: 11, 17, 18
to Tinghuset

Oslo Konserthus (Oslo Concert Hall)

Opened in 1977, the Oslo Concert Hall is home to the Oslo Philharmonic
Orchestra. It is also the leading venue for concerts and musical
productions in the city, with more than 300 events staged here
annually. The building was specially designed to present orchestral
works, and the podium is large enough to accommodate 120 musicians
at any one time. Ⓐ Munkedamsveien 14, public entrance from
Ruseløkkveien Ⓣ 23 11 31 00 Ⓦ www.oslokonserthus.no Ⓝ T-bane;
tram: 13, 19 to Nationaltheatret or 12 to Vikatorget

Oslo Nye Teater (Oslo New Theatre)

Some of Oslo's more urbane and modern theatre presentations
are staged here. Productions are held at three locations:
Hovedscenen in Rosenkrantz Gate, the Centralteateret in Akersgata
and the Trikkestallen puppet theatre in Torshovgata. Ⓐ Rosenkrantz
Gate 10 Ⓣ 22 34 86 80 Ⓦ www.oslonye.no (Norwegian only)
Ⓝ T-bane: Stortinget

Stenersenmuseet (Stenersen Museum)

The Stenersen Museum is named after author and art collector
Rolf Stenersen, who in 1936 donated his entire collection to the
city of Oslo. It was not until 1994 that the collection was removed
from storage and placed in this museum, along with the private
collections of Amaldus Nielsen and Ludvig Ravensberg, two of
Norway's more prominent artists. The collection includes paintings
and drawings by Edvard Munch, a close friend of Stenersen, Kai Fjell

and Jakob Weidemann. ❸ Munkedamsveien 15 ❶ 23 49 36 00
Ⓦ www.stenersen.museum.no ⏱ 11.00–19.00 Tues & Thur, 11.00–17.00
Wed, Fri–Sun, closed Mon Ⓜ T-bane; tram: 13, 19 to Nationaltheatret
❶ Admission charge

RETAIL THERAPY

The area around Karl Johans Gate is pedestrian-friendly and home
to shopping centres and department stores. You won't have any
problem finding a souvenir or gifts.

Bare Jazz Centrally located jazz café and record store that's
a treasure trove for jazz lovers. ❸ Grensen 8 ❶ 22 33 20 80
Ⓦ www.barejazz.no (Norwegian only) ⏱ 10.00–18.00 Mon & Tues,
10.00–24.00 Wed–Sat, closed Sun Ⓜ T-bane to Stortinget; tram: 11,
12, 13, 17, 18, 19 to Jernbanetorget

Byporten Adjacent to Central Station, this mega-mall has more than
70 stores, including fashion, sport and toy shops. Cafés and
restaurants are on hand for post-retail refreshment. ❸ Jernbanetorget 6
❶ 23 36 21 60 Ⓦ www.byporten.no (Norwegian only) ⏱ 10.00–21.00
Mon–Fri, 10.00–20.00 Sat, closed Sun Ⓜ T-bane; tram: 11, 12, 13, 17, 18,
19 to Jernbanetorget

Galleri Format Over 300 Norwegian artists are represented at this
shop, which sells all kinds of handicrafts in all manner of materials,
including ceramic, glass, metal and wood. It's worth a look if only
to browse the art exhibitions. ❸ Rådhusgata 24 ❶ 22 41 45 40
Ⓦ www.format.no (Norwegian only) ⏱ 11.00–17.00 Tues–Fri, 11.00–
16.00 Sat, 12.00–16.00 Sun Ⓜ Tram: 11, 13, 19 to Dronningensgate

GlasMagasinet One of the biggest department stores in Norway, it's a major outlet for Hadeland Glassverk, prime Norwegian glassware. An excellent coffee shop and restaurant are also on-site. ⓐ Stortorvet 9 ⓣ 22 03 20 80 ⓛ 10.00–19.00 Mon–Fri, 10.00–18.00 Sat, closed Sun ⓝ Tram: 11, 17, 18 to Stortorvet

House of Oslo Since it opened in 2006, this store has displayed the latest in Scandinavian interior design with kitchen, textiles, furniture and lighting departments over four floors. Featured names include Illums Bolighus and Room. You won't be able to fit a sofa in your suitcase, but a candlestick or a tablecloth might be a good souvenir. ⓐ Ruseløkkveien 26 ⓣ 23 23 85 60 ⓛ 10.00–20.00 Mon–Fri, 10.00–18.00 Sat, closed Sun ⓝ Tram: 12 to Vikatorvet

Juhls Silvergallery The design of the beautiful, unique jewellery sold here is inspired by the traditions of the Sami people in northern Norway. ⓐ Roald Amundsens Gate 6 ⓣ 22 42 77 99 ⓦ www.juhls.no ⓛ 10.00–17.00 Mon–Fri, 10.00–15.00 Sat, closed Sun ⓝ T-bane; tram: 13, 19 to Nationaltheatret

Norway Designs Clothes, jewellery, paper – you name it: anything with a Norwegian twist can be found here. ⓐ Stortingsgata 28 ⓣ 23 11 45 10 ⓦ www.norwaydesigns.no (Norwegian only) ⓛ 09.00–17.00 Mon–Wed & Fri, 11.00–19.00 Thur, 10.00–16.00 Sat, closed Sun ⓝ T-bane; tram: 13, 19 to Nationaltheatret

Oslo City A shopping centre close to Central Station, with plenty of fashion, book and home furnishings stores. ⓐ Stenersgata 1 ⓣ 81 54 40 33 ⓛ 10.00–22.00 Mon–Fri, 10.00–20.00 Sat, closed Sun ⓝ T-bane; tram: 11, 12, 13, 17, 18, 19 to Jernbanetorget

Paleet Come here to admire the bronze statue of Norwegian skating heroine Sonja Henje, and then shop in the upmarket complex of 45 stores. Handy if the weather's bad and you need somewhere to shelter. ⊜ Karl Johans Gate 37–43 ✆ 22 41 26 30 🕓 10.00–20.00 Mon–Fri, 10.00–18.00 Sat, closed Sun Ⓝ T-bane; tram: 13, 19 to Nationaltheatret

TAKING A BREAK

Steamen £ ❶ A maritime-themed pavement café with big windows in the Hotel Continental, conveniently situated next door to the National Theatre and good for people-watching whatever the weather. ⊜ Stortingsgata 24–26 ✆ 22 82 41 74 🌐 www.hotel continental.no 🕓 12.00–03.30 Wed–Sat, 12.00–01.30 Sun–Tues (May–Sept); 12.00–03.00 Wed–Sat, 12.00–01.00 Sun–Tues (Oct–May) Ⓝ T-bane; tram: 13, 19 to Nationaltheatret

Hambro's Café ££ ❷ One of the classiest coffee shops in the city, with subtle colours and antique furnishings. Choose from all sorts of goodies from the bakery, including filled ciabattas and luscious pastries. They also offer a variety of hot dishes. ⊜ Rosenkrantz Gate 3 ✆ 22 82 60 22 🕓 11.00–16.00 Mon & Tues, 11.00–22.00 Wed–Fri, 12.00–21.30 Sat, closed Sun Ⓝ Tram: 11, 17, 18 to Tinghuset

Grand Café £££ ❸ Ibsen is said to have had lunch at this café every day. It's a bit pricey, but worth it for the atmosphere – not to mention the cake buffet. ⊜ Karl Johans Gate 31 ✆ 23 21 20 00 🌐 www.grand.no 🕓 07.00–23.00 Mon–Sat, 07.00–22.00 Sun Ⓝ T-bane; tram: 13, 19 to Nationaltheatret

● *Do as Ibsen did and lunch at the Grand Café*

AFTER DARK

RESTAURANTS

TGI Friday's ££ ❹ Yes, it's an American chain with predictable ribs and steaks, but it's affordable and lively. The newest branch is conveniently between the cathedral and the main station. ⓐ Biskop Gunnerus' gate 3 ❶ 40 01 34 00 ⓦ www.fridays.no ⓛ 11.00–22.00 Sun–Wed, 11.00–23.00 Thur–Sat ⓣ T-bane: Jernbanetorget

Enzo Bar & Restaurant £££ ❺ Located in the Radisson Blu Scandinavia, this restaurant offers Norwegian ingredients cooked

Mediterranean-style. It's also a nice place just for a drink.
ⓐ Holbergsgate 30 ⓣ 23 29 30 00 ⓦ www.radissonblu.com/
scandinaviahotel-oslo ⓛ 09.00–23.00 Mon–Sat, 10.00–22.00 Sun
ⓝ Tram: 11, 17, 18 to Holbergs plass

Lofoten Fiskerestaurant £££ ❻ The outdoor tables at this restaurant
are perfect for a summer evening. The décor is modern and stylish,
and the excellent fish menu changes seasonally. ⓐ Stranden 75
ⓣ 22 83 08 08 ⓦ www.lofoten-fiskerestaurant.no ⓛ 11.00–23.00
Mon–Sat, 12.00–22.00 Sun ⓝ Tram: 12 to Aker Brygge; bus: 54 to
Aker Brygge

Theatercaféen £££ ❼ This restaurant in the Hotel Continental
opened in 1901 and, more than 100 years later, retains an
authentic turn-of-the-20th-century flair. It has been a haven for
many of Norway's notables, including Edvard Munch and Knut
Hamsun. ⓐ Stortingsgata 24–26 ⓣ 22 82 40 00 ⓦ www.hotel
continental.no ⓛ 11.00–23.00 Mon–Sat, 15.00–22.00 Sun ⓝ T-bane;
tram: 13, 19 to Nationaltheatret

BARS & CLUBS

34 Skybar Will it be the breathtaking views or the designer Martinis
that you remember the most? There's only one way to find out. It's
also worth stopping by during the day for a tapas lunch. ⓐ Radisson
Blu Plaza Hotel, Sonja Henies Plass 3 ⓣ 22 05 80 34 ⓛ 17.00–01.00
Mon–Thur, 17.00–01.30 Fri & Sat, closed Sun ⓝ T-bane; tram: 11, 12, 13,
17, 18, 19 to Jernbanetorget

Cafè Sør A relaxed, arty place which attracts a young crowd. A DJ
plays most nights and there are live performances from time to

⬤ *A central pavement café awaits the throngs*

time. 🚊 Torggata 11 ☎ 41 46 30 47 🌐 www.cafesor.no (Norwegian only) Ⓝ Tram: 11, 17, 18 to Stortorvet

Etoile Bar Set above the city on the seventh floor of the Rica Grand Hotel (see page 36), this charming bar is a lovely place for a nightcap. 🚊 Karl Johans Gate 31 ☎ 23 21 20 00 🌐 www.grand.no 🕐 10.00–01.00 Mon–Thur, 10.00–02.00 Fri & Sat, closed Sun Ⓝ T-bane; tram: 13, 19 to Nationaltheatret

Icebar Created from 50 tonnes of River Torne ice and serving Scandinavian cocktails in ice glasses, you won't need your vodka on the rocks in this bar. Entrance is every hour on the hour for a 45-minute session and booking is recommended. 🚊 Kristian IV's Gate 12 ☎ 22 42 66 61 🌐 www.icebar.no 🕐 15.00–24.00 Mon–Thur, 15.00–01.00 Fri, 12.00–01.00 Sat, closed Sun Ⓝ T-bane; tram 13, 19 to Nationaltheatret

Luna Park A quiet, calm bar, perfect for a drink and a chat with a good friend. Tasty tapas and pizzas are served until 23.30 Sun–Wed and 02.30 Thur–Sat. ❸ Badstugata 1 ❶ 22 20 82 55 Ⓦ www.luna parkoslo.no (Norwegian only) ❻ 16.00–03.30 daily Ⓝ T-bane: Jernbanetorget

Onkel Donald One of Oslo's hotspots, this café-bar combines really good Norwegian food with a chic atmosphere. Late at night it changes from an eatery to a bar. ❸ Universitetsgata 26 ❶ 23 35 63 10 ❻ 12.00–24.00 Mon–Thur, 12.00–03.00 Fri & Sat, closed Sun Ⓝ T-bane; tram: 13, 19 to Nationaltheatret

Sikamikanico DJs of all types set an ever-changing tone at Sikamikanico, one of the city's best club scenes. ❸ Møllergata 2 ❶ 22 41 44 09 Ⓦ www.sikamikanico.net (Norwegian only) ❻ 21.00–03.30 Wed & Thur, 14.00–03.30 Fri & Sat, 10.00–03.30 Sun, closed Mon & Tues Ⓝ Tram: 11, 17, 18 to Stortorvet

Summit Enjoy the view along with your cocktail at this 21st-storey hotel bar with its stunning vista over the city. ❸ Holbergsgate 30 ❶ 23 29 30 00 Ⓦ www.radissonblu.com/scandinaviahotel-oslo ❻ 16.00–01.00 Mon–Thur, 16.00–02.30 Fri & Sat, 17.00–01.00 Sun Ⓝ Tram: 11, 17, 18 to Holbergs plass

Yatzi A two-storey nightclub, restaurant and lounge in one, so whether you want to dance the night away or simply relax with a drink this is the place to go. ❸ Nedre Slottsgate 2 ❶ 22 42 99 50 Ⓦ www.yatzi.no ❻ 15.00–03.00 Fri, 23.00–03.00 Sat, closed Sun–Thur Ⓝ Bus: 60 to Bankplassen

Grünerløkka & Grønland

Two pockets of eastern Oslo have rapidly been emerging as dynamic multicultural areas with an impressive array of nightlife and eateries. Grünerløkka has changed from a dingy and rundown part of town, mostly home to the city's immigrants, into a trend-setting district. The cafés and restaurants have started to outgrow the area and have spilled into neighbouring Grønland. For locations of listings in this section, see the main city map on pages 52–3.

CULTURE

Kunstindustrimuseet (Museum of Applied Art)

The Museum of Applied Art, established in 1876, is one of the oldest of its kind in Europe. It houses a fine collection of Norwegian and foreign crafts and clothes from the 17th century to the present. The star of the collection is the Baldishol Tapestry, dating from 1200. This national treasure is the only surviving Norwegian tapestry that employed the Gobelin technique, and was only found when the Baldishole Church in Hedmark county was demolished in 1879. The museum also contains silver, ceramics and furniture. ❸ St Olavs Gate 1 ☎ 21 98 20 00 🖰 www.national museum.no 🕑 11.00–17.00 Tues, Wed, Fri, 11.00–19.00 Thur, 12.00–16.00 Sat & Sun, closed Mon 🚇 T-bane; tram: 13, 19 to Nationaltheatret; bus: 33, 37, 46 to Nordahl Bruns Gate

Munch-museet (Munch Museum)

The Munch Museum houses the world's largest collection of work by Edvard Munch. Just before his death, the artist bequeathed all the paintings in his possession to the city. The collection is massive,

🔺 *The Oslo Spektrum hosts all the big names*

containing some 1,100 paintings, 4,500 drawings and 18,000 prints. On display are several versions of *The Scream*, his best-known work. In 2004, following the theft of one of only two painted versions of *The Scream* (as well as *Madonna*), the museum was closed for months while security was upgraded, but the paintings are once again on display to the public. Many of Munch's other paintings are frequently on loan to other museums, but with over 180 sq m (1,937 sq ft) of exhibition space you won't feel deprived. Plans for a new museum have recently stalled. 🚋 Tøyengata 53 📞 23 49 35 00 🌐 www.munch.museum.no 🕐 10.00–18.00 daily (June–Aug); 10.00–16.00 Tues, Wed, Fri & Sat, 10.00–20.00 Thur, 11.00–17.00 Sun, closed Mon (Sept–May) 🚇 T-bane: Tøyen; bus: 20 to Munch Museet ⓘ Admission charge

Oslo Spektrum

A venue for big concerts, cultural and sporting events, this is where the Nobel Peace Prize Concert, the Norwegian Military Tattoo and the

Oslo Horse Show are held. International artists including Eminem, Britney Spears and Metallica have also performed here. ❷ Sonja Henies Plass 2 ❶ Information: 22 05 29 00; tickets: 81 51 12 11 ❿ www.oslospektrum.no ❻ Tram: 18, 19 to Bussterminalen Grønland

RETAIL THERAPY

The once working-class area by the Akerselva River has over the last decade become one of the most interesting areas of Oslo. The atmosphere generated by so many immigrant nationalities, such as Pakistani and Somali, is both electric and eclectic. Take some time to discover the numerous small shops and delicatessens. The best hunting ground is the area near the main streets of Markveien and Thorvald Meyers Gate.

Conzept A small shop selling unique – and beautiful – jewellery. If you are not completely happy with the pieces on display, the staff will adjust or redesign them for you. ❷ Steenstrupgate 12 ❶ 22 35 09 00 ❹ 10.00–18.00 Mon–Fri, 10.00–16.00 Sat, 12.00–16.00 Sun ❻ Tram: 11, 12, 13 to Olaf Ryes plass

Grønland Basar You can't miss the striking entrance to this shopping arcade, which contains mostly individual, ethnic-style shops. ❷ Tøyengata 2–6 ❶ 22 17 05 71 ❹ 10.00–20.00 Mon–Fri, 10.00–18.00 Sat, closed Sun ❻ T-bane: Grønland

Sjarm A cute little store, with a bit of everything – shoes, interior design and decorations. It's also open on Sundays. ❷ Sofienberggata 6 ❶ 22 37 19 32 ❹ 10.00–18.30 Mon–Wed & Fri, 10.00–19.00 Thur, 10.00–18.00 Sat, 12.00–18.00 Sun ❻ Tram 11, 12, 13 to Olaf Ryes plass

TAKING A BREAK

Bør & Børsen £ ❶ Offering that rare thing in Oslo – a bargain – this simple, informal place has a menu that includes pasta, steaks and pizzas, with the dish of the day usually less than 100Kr. There's karaoke at the weekends and sports on big screens.
ⓐ Trondheimsveien 13 ❶ 22 68 86 48 🕐 14.00–03.00 daily

Hotel Havana £ ❷ A quirky delicatessen selling lots of exotic munchies.
ⓐ Thorvald Meyers Gate 36 ❶ 23 23 03 23 🕐 10.00–18.00 Mon–Sat, closed Sun Ⓝ Tram: 11, 12, 13 to Olaf Ryes plass

Kaffebrenneriet £ ❸ A great place for a breather. Try a fresh juice, or the coffee of the day with a brownie – always a winner.
ⓐ Grønlandsleiret 32 ❶ 22 46 13 90 🕐 07.00–19.00 Mon–Fri, 09.00–17.00 Sat, 10.00–17.00 Sun Ⓝ T-bane: Grønland

Fru Hagen £–££ ❹ A trendy, arty sort of place serving international dishes until 21.30, when it turns into an upmarket bar. Be prepared for a long wait for an outside table during the summer. ⓐ Thorvald Meyers Gate 40 ❶ 45 49 19 04 🕐 11.00–24.00 Mon & Tues, 11.00–02.00 Wed, 11.00–03.00 Thur–Sat, 12.00–23.00 Sun Ⓝ Tram: 11, 12, 13 to Olaf Ryes plass

Mucho Mas £–££ ❺ It doesn't look much from the outside, but the food here is top-notch Mexican. You'll find tacos, burritos, nachos and plenty of beer to put out the fire from too many *chiles rellenos*.
ⓐ Thorvald Meyers Gate 36 ❶ 22 37 16 09 Ⓦ www.muchomas.no 🕐 12.00–24.00 or 01.00 daily (times vary) Ⓝ Tram: 11, 12, 13 to Olaf Ryes plass

AFTER DARK

RESTAURANTS

Punjab Tandoori £ ❻ Samosas, dhal and tasty curries that aren't too hot (unless you ask for them that way) make for a filling and not-too-expensive meal very near the T-bane station. ❸ Grønland 24 ❶ 22 17 20 86 ❺ 11.00–23.00 Mon–Sat, 11.00–22.00 Sun ❻ T-bane: Grønland

Bistro Brocante ££–£££ ❼ An excellent choice if you're in the mood for French cuisine. In summer this Parisian-style bistro has outdoor tables, which are always at a premium. ❸ Thorvald Meyers Gate 40 ❶ 22 35 68 71 ❺ 11.00–24.00 daily ❻ Tram: 11, 12, 13 to Olaf Ryes plass

Sult £££ ❽ A highly popular and informal restaurant that's always filled with hungry diners waiting to plough into platefuls of pasta and fish. Get there early or be prepared to wait. ❸ Thorvald Meyers Gate 26 ❶ 67 10 99 70 ❺ 17.00–22.00 Mon–Fri, 13.00–22.00 Sat, 13.00–20.00 Sun ❻ Tram: 11, 12, 13 to Olaf Ryes plass

BARS & CLUBS

Bar Boca Call it small or intimate, this bar with its 1950s-inspired interior is without doubt one of the coolest venues in Grünerløkka. Probably the best Bloody Mary in town, too. ❸ Thorvald Meyers Gate 30 ❶ 41 16 41 16 ❺ 12.00–01.00 Sun–Tues, 12.00–02.00 Wed & Thur, 12.00–03.00 Fri & Sat ❻ Tram: 11, 12, 13 to Olaf Ryes plass

Blå Hosts a mix of live music and different club nights. ❸ Brenneriveien 9C ❶ 98 25 63 86 ❿ www.blaaoslo.no (Norwegian only) ❺ Outdoor tables: 13.00–24.00 Mon–Fri, 12.00–24.00 Sat & Sun; club: 21.00–03.30 daily ❻ Tram: 11, 17, 18 to Stortorvet

 *Grünerløkka's hotspot number one, Bar Boca*

Café Kaos Another addition to Grünerløkka's ever-expanding music scene. Great for the summer, with its large outside area. ⓐ Thorvald Meyers Gate 56 ⓣ 22 04 69 90 ⓦ www.cafekaos.no (Norwegian only) ⓛ 17.00–03.30 Mon–Sat, 20.00–03.00 Sun ⓜ Tram: 11, 12, 13 to Olaf Ryes plass

Gloria Flames A bar with a roof garden – the perfect combination for a hot summer's night. ⓐ Grønland 18 ⓣ 22 17 16 00 ⓛ 18.00–02.00 Tues–Thur, 15.00–03.00 Fri & Sat, closed Sun & Mon ⓜ T-bane: Grønland

Parkteatret Bar og Scene This is one of the trendiest places in town – but be prepared to queue. ⓐ Olaf Ryes plass 11 ⓣ Club: 22 35 63 00; bar: 93 28 80 02 ⓦ www.parkteatret.no ⓛ 11.00–01.00 Sun–Tues, 11.00–02.00 Wed & Thur, 11.00–03.00 Fri & Sat ⓜ Tram: 11, 12, 13 to Olaf Ryes plass

Bygdøy Peninsula

Bygdøy was an island until the end of the 19th century, when the sound between Frognerkilen and Bestumkilen was filled. Today this area is home to some of the finest museums and attractions Oslo has to offer. The peninsula is easy to access in summer – just take the ferry that runs from the quay opposite Rådhuset. There are also frequent bus connections from the city centre. In addition to cultural sights, the area is covered with meadows and parklands filled with a wealth of plant species, and in summer the beaches are a popular place to escape to.

SIGHTS & ATTRACTIONS

Hukodden

This hook-shaped promontory is home to Paradisbukta (which translates as Paradise Bay), perhaps the best beach and seaside park in Oslo. Because it is easily accessible from the city, Hukodden teems with bathers on weekends. But if lying sardine-style on the beach isn't for you, there are plenty of pleasant strolls to be had on the walkways along the shore and through the adjoining woods. From the furthest point on the Huk, or 'head', you'll get a terrific view of the Oslo fjord, stretching from the Dyna lighthouse to Nesoddtangen in the south. If you prefer to sunbathe au naturel, head for the naturist beach to the north of Paradise Bay. The bay is only a 15-minute walk from the museums of Bygdøy, and there's a restaurant open in the summer months. ❷ Hukodden Beach Restaurant, Strømsborgveien 46 M ❶ 22 43 74 62 ❷ Bus: 30 to Bygdøynes; ferry: 91 from Rådhuskaia (City Hall Quay) to Bygdøynes (May–Sept only)

Bygdøy Peninsula

0   250 metres
0   250 yards

SKØYEN

Vigelandsparken
Vigeland Monolitten

Frognerdammene

KIRKEVEIEN

Majorstuen M

MIDDELTHUNS GT

Frognerparken

DAHLS GT

MUNTHES GT

Oslo Bymuseum

HALVDAN SVARTES GT

Vigeland-
museet

NORDRAKS GT
GYLDENLØVES GT
TIDEMANDS GT
ECKERSBERGS GT

FROGNER

DRAMMENSVEIEN

MESSEVEIEN

NEDRE SKØYEN VEI

ASKEVEIEN

PRINSESSA

GUSTAV VIGELANDS VEI

HJORTNESV.

THORVALD ERICHSENSVEI

MAJORSTUD ALLÉ

KRISTINELUNDVEIEN

HAFRSFJORDS GT
NOBELS GT

BYGDØY ALLÉ

ODINS GT
ELISENBERGVEIEN

GIMLEVEIEN

LØVENSKIOLDS GT

FROGNERVN.

O. KYRRES GT

FRONS GT

DRAMMENSVEIEN

LIBES GT
GABELS GT
HEFTYES GT

BYGDØY ALLÉ

M THORSENS GT
NIELS JUELS GT

NILS JUELS GT
MUNKEDAMSVN.

DRONNING BLANCAS VEI

BYGDØYVEIEN

Frognerkilen

Frognerstranda

DRAMMENSVEIEN

BYGDØY

N

Oscarshall

OSCARSHALLVEIEN

WEDELS VEI

MUSEUMSVEIEN

DRONNINGHAVNVEIEN

MELLBYEDALEN

HUK AVENY

➋ DRONNINGEN

📷 Dronningen
ferry pier

Norske
Folkemuseum

Vikingskipshuset

LANGVIKSVEIEN

C BENNECHES VEI

HUK AVENY

Langvikbukta

Rådhuskaia

Kon-Tiki Museet

LØCHENVEIEN

Frammuseet

📷 Bygdøynes
ferry pier

Norsk Maritimt Museum

▓ ......POI
M ......T-bane Stop
📷 ......Port

➊ ←

Villa
Grande

Hukodden

BYGDØYNESVEIEN

Sjømannskirken
Bygdøy

Oslofjorden

Oscarshall

Every king needs a place to get away from it all, and 19th-century King Oscar I was no exception. This residence was originally conceived as a showcase of the architecture, art and handicrafts of the country. The 19th-century castle is Norway's finest neo-Gothic building and was reopened in 2009 after extensive renovation. Terraces with fountains lead down to the sea. Visiting is by guided tour only, from the end of August to the end of September; at other times of the year, you can simply admire it from the outside. ⓐ Oscarshallveien 805, Bygdøy ⓣ 22 56 15 39 ⓦ www.kongehuset.no ⓛ Tour times vary; call for information ⓝ Bus: 30 to Kongsgården

Sjømannskirken Bygdøy (Sailors' Church)

This is the Oslo Seamen's Mission, devoted to those who work on the ships in the port of Oslo and used as a social centre. The grounds are home to the Seamen's Memorial, which was erected in 1966 to commemorate all the Norwegian sailors who have perished at sea. ⓐ Admiral Børresens vei 4 ⓣ 22 43 82 90 ⓝ Bus: 30 to Herbernveien

CULTURE

Frammuseet (Fram Museum)

Opposite the Kon-Tiki Museum is the Fram Museum, home of the polar ship *Fram*. Dating from 1892 and billed as 'the world's strongest ship', she has sailed to the North Pole and the far reaches of Antarctica. Used by explorers Nansen and Amundsen on their expeditions, the ship has been on display since 1936. In 2011, to celebrate the centenaries of Nansen's birth and Amundsen's South Pole expedition, and the 75th anniversary of the museum itself, the buildings were renovated and the displays updated with new

⬥ *This cart is part of the Viking heritage on display at Frammuseet*

exhibitions. By the end of 2012, the explorers' ship *Gjøa* will be
housed in her own building and the whole site will become a
comprehensive museum of polar exploration, with *Fram* as its star.
🅐 Bygdøynesveien 36 📞 23 28 29 50 🅦 www.frammuseum.no
🕐 10.00–16.00 daily (Mar–Apr & Oct); 10.00–17.00 daily (May &
Sept); 09.00–18.00 daily (June–Aug); 10.00–15.00 Mon–Fri,
10.00–16.00 Sat & Sun (Nov–Feb) 🅐 Bus: 30 to Bygdøynes; ferry: 91
from Rådhuskaia (City Hall Quay) to Bygdøynes (May–Sept only)
🅘 Admission charge

Kon-Tiki Museet (Kon-Tiki Museum)

Thor Heyerdahl held the world's interest in 1947 when he sailed his balsawood raft *Kon-Tiki* across the vast reaches of the South Pacific to prove that it would have been possible for South Americans to reach Polynesia by boat. The raft and artefacts from this and other voyages are on display here along with fascinating objects from Easter Island, which include a 10-m (33-ft)-high statue and a re-created 30-m (100-ft)-deep cave. There's also a short film about Heyerdahl's voyage, played on a loop. ➌ Bygdøynesveien 36 ☎ 23 08 67 67 ⓦ www.kon-tiki.no ⏱ 10.00–16.00 daily (Nov–Feb); 10.00–17.00 daily (Mar–May & Sept–Oct); 09.00–18.00 daily (June–Aug) Ⓑ Bus: 30 to Bygdøynes; ferry: 91 from Rådhuskaia (City Hall Quay) to Bygdøynes (May–Sept only) ⓘ Admission charge

Norske Folkemuseum (Norwegian Folk Museum)

More than 150 buildings gathered from all over Norway have been assembled here to create Europe's largest open-air museum. Wander through centuries of everyday history via farmhouses, market streets and churches; there's even a petrol station from the 1920s. The Gol Stave Church, adorned with paintings and carvings, has survived from 1200 and is one of 30 such preserved churches in the country. Costumed guides play their roles well, while annual events include the Midsummer Eve celebration, and the Christmas market in December. ➌ Museumsveien 10, Bygdøy ☎ 22 12 37 00 ⓦ www.norskfolkemuseum.no ⏱ 10.00–18.00 daily (mid-May–mid-Sept); 11.00–15.00 Mon–Fri, 10.00–16.00 Sat & Sun (mid-Sept–mid-May) Ⓑ Bus: 30 to Bygdøynes; ferry: 91 from Rådhuskaia (City Hall Quay) to Dronningen (May–Sept only) ⓘ Admission charge

◯ The quaint Gol Stave Church is one of the stars of the Norske Folkemuseum

Norsk Maritimt Museum (Norwegian Maritime Museum)

From the elegant ships of the early Viking explorers to the latter-day supertankers, Norway has always been at the forefront of marine activity. Completing the trio of institutions in this corner of Bygdøy is this museum displaying the history and traditions of Norwegian fishing, shipbuilding and marine archaeology.

Some parts of the premises will be temporarily closed for renovation in the lead-up to 2014, when a renovated and restored museum will celebrate its hundredth anniversary. However, the new exhibits will open as they are finished, so there will still be plenty to see. ❸ Bygdøynesveien 37 ❶ 24 11 41 50 ❿ www.marmuseum.no ⏰ 10.00–18.00 daily (mid-May–Aug); 10.00–15.00 Tues–Fri, 10.00–16.00 Sat & Sun, closed Mon (Sept–late May) ❿ Bus: 30 to

🔺 *The exterior of the Viking Ship Museum gives no hint of the treasures within*

Bygdøynes; ferry: 91 from Rådhuskaia (City Hall Quay) to Bygdøynes (May–Sept only) ❶ Admission charge

Vikingskipshuset (Viking Ship Museum)

This museum houses the world's best-preserved Viking ships. Built in the 9th century, the two burial ships are an impressive sight. The museum is also home to Viking-era small boats, sledges, an ornately decorated cart and household gear. ❸ Huk Aveny 35, Bygdøy ❶ 22 13 52 80 🅦 www.khm.uio.no 🕒 09.00–18.00 Tues–Sun, closed Mon (May–Sept); 10.00–16.00 Tues–Sun, closed Mon (Oct–Apr) 🚍 Bus: 30 to Vikingskipshuset; ferry: 91 from Rådhuskaia (City Hall Quay) to Dronningen (May–Sept only) ❶ Admission charge

◔ *Heroic figures at the Maritime Museum*

Villa Grande

The former residence of Norwegian Nazi collaborator Vidkun Quisling has been turned into a Holocaust centre, with a permanent exhibition on the Holocaust and other genocides. Displays include sound, film, photos and artefacts. ⓐ Huk Aveny 56 ⓣ 22 84 21 00 ⓦ www.hlsenteret.no ⓛ 10.00–18.00 (last admission 17.00) daily ⓝ Bus: 30 to Bygdøynes; ferry: 91 from Rådhuskaia (City Hall Quay) to Dronningen (May–Sept only) ⓘ Admission charge

RETAIL THERAPY

The best bets for shopping in the Bygdøy area are the gift stores in the various museums, which are filled to the brim with Norwegian handicrafts. In December the Christmas market at the Norske Folkemuseum is not to be missed.

TAKING A BREAK

Sult Hukodden ££ ❶ This restaurant is only open during the summer season, and offers fresh seafood and tasty lunches. ⓐ Strømsborgveien 46 M ⓣ 22 43 74 62 ⓛ From 12.00 daily (May–Sept only) ⓝ Bus: 30 to Bygdøy Huk; ferry: 91 from Rådhuskaia (City Hall Quay) to Bygdøynes (May–Sept only)

Lanternen Restaurant £££ ❷ The owners of this place must be sun-seekers: it's only open in summer, and the sunnier it is, the longer it stays open. Hours given below are for the earliest closing time. ⓐ Huk Aveny 2 ⓣ 22 43 78 38 ⓛ 11.30–20.30 Mon–Sat, 13.00–19.00 Sun (Apr–Oct only) ⓝ Bus: 30 to Bygdøynes; ferry: 91 from Rådhuskaia (City Hall Quay) to Dronningen (May–Sept only)

Holmenkollen, Frogner & Majorstua

Much of what Oslo has to offer is located to the northwest of the city centre. Whether it's the sculptures in Vigeland Park, the new ski jump at Holmenkollen, or the many museums in the suburbs, you'll want to allow some time to visit them. Label-conscious party animals will feel right at home in the West End atmosphere of Majorstua and Frogner, while Bogstadveien and Hegdehaugsveien have an abundance of bars and pubs that stay open long into the night. Thankfully, Oslo's efficient public transport system makes it easy to get to all of these places.

SIGHTS & ATTRACTIONS

Bærums Verk

Set in an ironworks dating from 1610, this market is a good place to come for unique handicrafts. If you get tired of shopping, you can always wander around the museum. Part of the market is also open on Sunday afternoons. ❷ Verksgata 15 ❶ 67 13 00 18 ❿ www.baerums verk.no ❺ 10.00–20.00 Mon–Fri, 10.00–18.00 Sat ❻ Bus: 753, 143 to Bærums Verk

Bogstad Gård (Bogstad Manor)

An 18th-century farming estate lying on the eastern bank of Bogstad Lake, Bogstad Herregård dates back to the Middle Ages. It was owned by a series of famous and wealthy Norwegians before becoming an extension of the Norske Folkemuseum in 1955. The current manor house was built in the late 1700s by Peder Anker, who went on to become prime minister. Most of the artwork and other artefacts date to that time, as do the beautiful English-style

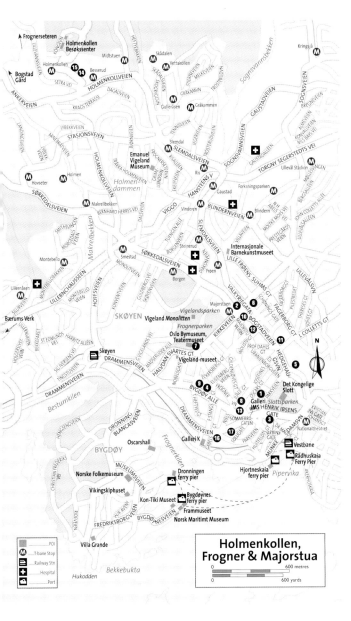

Holmenkollen, Frogner & Majorstua

0   600 metres

0   600 yards

Legend
- POI
- Ⓜ T-bane Stop
- Railway Stn
- Hospital
- Port

park and gardens surrounding the estate. There is a café and a shop on-site. ❷ Sørkedalen 826 ☎ 22 06 52 00 ⓦ www.bogstad.no ⏰ 12.00–16.00 Tues–Sun, closed Mon ⓝ Bus: 32 to Røa, then 41 to Bogstad Gård ⓘ Admission charge

Frognerseteren

This recreational area near Holmenkollen is the starting point for well-marked hiking and skiing trails in the Nordmarka woods. Originally inhabited in 1790, it became public at the end of the 19th century when a traditional wooden lodge was built, which now houses the restaurant. From the observation tower you can see Oslo, the Oslofjorden and even Sweden. ❷ Holmenkollveien 200 ☎ 22 92 40 40 ⏰ 11.00–22.00 Mon–Sat, 11.00–21.00 Sun ⓝ T-bane: Frognerseteren

Holmenkollen Besøkssenter

The Holmenkollen ski jump, the world's first designer ski jump, was revamped for the World Ski Championships in 2011. Illuminated at night, Holmenkollenbakken, as it is known in Norwegian, can be seen from all over the city and is the world's most modern such facility, with room for some 30,000 spectators. If you want to know what it's like to jump off one of the world's toughest hills, try the Holmenkollen ski simulator (☎ 95 09 71 20). Inside the jump itself, the Ski Museum, which first opened in 1923 and is the world's oldest, was also renovated and new displays cover the history of the activity from 4,000 years ago to the present day. Holmenkollen has three souvenir shops, a café with a terrace that has a view of the city, as well as free parking and toilets. If you choose not to visit the tower, you can also get good views from the outdoor areas around the jump. Among the activities available in the area are cycling, cross-country skiing and slalom. ❷ Kongeveien 5 ☎ 91 67 19 46

Ⓦ www.holmenkollen.com or www.skiforeningen.no Ⓛ 10.00–17.00 daily (May & Sept); 09.00–20.00 daily (June–Aug); 10.00–16.00 daily (Oct–Apr) Ⓣ T-bane: Holmenkollen

● Share Vigeland's astonishing visions at the park named after him

Vigelandsparken (Vigeland Park)

Part of the much bigger Frogner Park, this, the world's largest sculpture park, is dedicated to sculptor Gustav Vigeland and contains 212 of his works. The centrepiece is the 17-m (53-ft)-high *Monolitten* (Monolith), with 121 human figures supporting each other. Other highlights are the bridge and the fountain. The park has tennis courts and an adjacent public swimming pool, both open only during the summer months. There's also a visitor centre and a café at the main entrance. ➌ Kirkeveien ➊ 23 49 37 00 ➍ www.vigeland. museum.no ➋ 24 hrs ➎ T-bane: Majorstuen; tram: 12 to Vigelandsparken

CULTURE

Emanuel Vigeland Museum

This unusual building was once the studio of Emanuel Vigeland, and is now his mausoleum as well as a museum (his ashes are in an urn over the entrance door). Renowned for his frescoes and stained glass, Emanuel also painted and sculpted. On display here is *Vita* (*Life*), a group of frescoes that were considered very risqué when they were produced in the 1940s. The museum is only open to the public on Sunday afternoons, but it is possible to book a private viewing during the week for an extra fee. ➌ Grimelundsveien 8 ➊ 22 14 57 88 ➍ www.emanuelvigeland.museum.no ➋ 12.00–17.00 Sun only (mid-May–mid-Sept); 12.00–16.00 Sun only (mid-Sept–mid-May) ➎ T-bane: Slemdal; bus: 46 to Grimelundsveien ➊ Admission charge

Internasjonale Barnekunstmuseet (International Museum of Children's Art)

Founded in 1986 in association with SOS Children's Villages and featuring children's art from over 150 countries, the museum is a showcase for paintings, sculptures, ceramics, textiles and collages. Children can participate in music, dance, painting and drawing, and there are also films, videos and workshops. The on-site shop is worth a browse. 🅐 Lille Frøens Vei 4 🅝 22 46 85 73 🅦 www.barnekunst.no 🅒 11.00–16.00 Tues–Thur & Sun, closed Mon, Fri & Sat (late June–mid-Aug); 09.30–14.00 Tues–Thur, 11.00–16.00 Sun, closed Mon, Fri & Sat (mid-Sept–late June); closed mid-Aug–mid-Sept 🅝 T-bane: Frøen 🅘 Admission charge

Oslo Bymuseum (Oslo City Museum)

Located in the Vigelandsparken, this 18th-century manor house is dedicated to the history of Oslo, with models, pictures, room interiors and displays. There are three other buildings, which together with the museum form a traditional farm layout with an open square in the middle. A café and shop are on-site, too. 🅐 Frogner Hovedgård (Frogner Manor), Frognerveien 67 🅝 23 28 41 70 🅦 www.oslomuseum.no 🅒 11.00–16.00 Tues–Sun, closed Mon 🅝 T-bane: Majorstuen; tram: 12 to Frogner plass

Teatermuseet (Theatre Museum)

Housed in the City Museum at Frogner Manor, this museum traces the history of theatre in Oslo from 1800 onwards. 🅐 Frognerveien 67 🅝 22 05 28 30 🅦 www.oslomuseum.no 🅒 11.00–16.00 Tues–Sun, closed Mon 🅝 Tram: 12 to Frogner plass

Vigeland-museet (Vigeland Museum)

The museum dedicated to Norway's great sculptor Gustav Vigeland lies just outside Vigelandsparken, and contains the majority of the artist's work – 1,600 sculptures and more than 10,000 drawings, woodcuts and carvings. It was built in Norwegian neoclassical style, initially as a studio for Vigeland on the understanding that it would eventually become a museum containing his work. His ashes are in the museum's tower. 🅰 Nobelsgate 32 🕐 23 49 37 00 🆆 www.vigeland.museum.no 🕑 11.00–17.00 Tues–Sun, closed Mon (June–Aug); 12.00–16.00 Tues–Sun, closed Mon (Sept–May) 🅝 T-bane: Majorstuen; tram: 12 to Frogner plass ❶ Admission charge (free Oct–Mar)

Private galleries

Galleri JMS One of the best galleries in Oslo for contemporary art, by both Norwegian and international artists. 🅰 Sommerrogaten 13–15 🕐 22 92 55 07 🆆 www.gallerijms.no 🕑 Times vary

Galleri K Owned by Ben Fria, a noted authority on the works of Edvard Munch and many other Norwegian artists. 🅰 Bjørn Farmannsgate 6, one block west of Gabels Gate 🕐 22 55 35 88 🆆 www.gallerik.com 🕑 11.00–16.00 Tues–Fri, 11.00–15.00 Sat, 12.00–15.00 Sun, closed Mon ❶ Times may vary, especially in summer, so call before visiting

RETAIL THERAPY

Between the Royal Palace and Vigeland Park is the retail shopping area of Majorstua. The best shops are on Hegdehaugsveien and Bogstadveien. Frogner is also home to designer clothing and furniture stores. For unusual gifts, check out the museum shops.

Amalies A well-chosen collection of high-quality Danish and Spanish brands such as Ilse Jacobsen and Desigual. 🅰 Bogstadveien 8 🕐 22 56 67 00 🕑 10.00–18.00 Mon–Wed & Fri, 10.00–19.00 Thur, 10.00–17.00 Sat, closed Sun 🅝 T-bane; tram: 11, 12, 19 to Majorstuen

Anton Sport Høyfjellsutstyr This sports equipment store has Norway's biggest selection of backpacks. Norwegian brands such as Sweet, Norrøna and Ajungilak all feature. ❷ Bogstadveien 1 ❶ 22 95 59 70 ❸ 09.00–18.00 Mon–Wed & Fri, 09.00–19.00 Thur, 09.00–17.00 Sat, closed Sun ❷ T-bane; tram: 11, 12, 19 to Majorstuen

Kamikaze Exclusive designer clothing for men and women who like to be at the cutting edge of style. ❷ Hegdehaugsveien 24 & 27 ❶ 22 60 20 25 ❸ 10.00–17.00 Mon–Wed, 10.00–18.00 Thur, 10.00–17.30 Fri, 10.00–15.30 Sat, closed Sun ❷ T-bane; tram: 11, 12, 19 to Majorstuen ❶ Closes 1 hr earlier than stated times in July

◆ Oslo's Karl Johan Gate

Lille Vinkel Sko Carries a range of young, trendy shoes. ❸ Valkyriegata 9 ❶ 23 36 79 65 ⓦ www.lillevinkelsko.no ⓛ 09.00–19.00 Mon–Fri, 10.00–17.00 Sat, closed Sun ⓝ T-bane; tram: 11, 12, 19 to Majorstuen

Sprell A fun store for kids of all ages, selling high-quality toys made from natural materials. ❸ Hegdehaugsveien 36 ❶ 23 22 22 22 ⓛ 10.00–18.00 Mon–Fri, 10.00–17.00 Sat, closed Sun

Tonica Vintage Corner As its name suggests, this store specialises in vintage clothes. ❸ Schøningsgate 14 ❶ 22 60 22 06 ⓛ 11.00–18.00 Wed–Sat, closed Sun ⓝ T-bane; tram: 11, 12, 19 to Majorstuen

TAKING A BREAK

Frogner and Majorstua offer a wide variety of cafés and restaurants, some fairly exclusive, and many catering to the young and trendy.

Åpent Bakeri £ ❶ Don't say we didn't warn you! The freshly baked bread and just-brewed coffee here are simply irresistible… so don't be surprised to find a queue out of the door and down the street. ❸ Inkognito Terasse 1, one block southeast of Oscars Gate ❶ 22 44 94 70 ⓛ 07.30–17.00 Mon–Fri, 08.00–15.00 Sat, closed Sun ⓝ T-bane; tram: 13, 19 to Nationaltheatret

Samson £ ❷ This traditional corner bakery-café is a nice place to stop and put your feet up for a bit in between rounds of sightseeing. ❸ Valkyriegata 8 ❶ 22 46 50 75 ⓛ 07.30–18.00 Mon–Fri, 09.00–16.30 Sat, 11.00–17.00 Sun ⓝ T-bane; tram: 11, 12, 19 to Majorstuen ❶ Closed Sun in summer

Pascal ££ ❸ Pascal's is famous for its pastries and cakes that border on being works of art. Bill Clinton stopped in to indulge in the goodies in the glass cases. ⓐ Henrik Ibsens Gate 36 ❶ 22 55 00 20 ⓒ 08.00–22.30 Mon–Fri, 10.00–22.30 Sat, 12.00–17.00 Sun Ⓝ T-bane; tram: 13, 19 to Nationaltheatret

Café Elise ££–£££ ❹ A cheerful and sunny little bistro with glass walls that let the light in. Limited menu, though. ⓐ Elisenbergveien 22, left off Bygdøy Allé one block southeast of Thomas Heftyes Gate ❶ 22 44 25 11 ⓒ 11.30–23.00 Mon–Sat, 13.30–22.00 Sun Ⓝ T-bane; tram: 13, 19 to Nationaltheatret; bus: 30 to Frogner Kirke

Lorry ££–£££ ❺ This two-storey restaurant practically doubles as a gallery, showcasing more than 270 pieces of art. The atmosphere is warm and inviting. ⓐ Parkveien 12 ❶ 22 69 69 04 Ⓦ www.lorry.no ⓒ 11.00–03.30 Mon–Sat, 12.00–01.30 Sun

Café M £££ ❻ A short walk from Vigelandsparken, this place has a bar/café area, as well as a full restaurant, plus outdoor seating in summer. ⓐ Valkyriegata 9 ❶ 22 60 34 00 ⓒ 11.00–22.30 Mon–Sat, 13.00–23.30 Sun Ⓝ T-bane; tram: 11, 12, 19 to Majorstuen

Herregårdskroen £££ ❼ In the Oslo Museum in Frogner Manor, Herregårdskroen is a good place to get away from the hustle and bustle of the city. Surrounded by open space, large trees and near Frogner Lake, it also has good views of the park. ⓐ Frognerveien 67 ❶ 22 43 77 30 ⓒ 10.00–22.00 daily (Easter–Sept) Ⓝ T-bane; tram: 11, 12, 19 to Majorstuen ❶ Shorter hours in wet weather

AFTER DARK

The Majorstua and Frogner areas of Oslo are the trendiest and most expensive parts of town. This is where you go to see and be seen. Dress your best and expect some long waits at the weekends, unless you've made reservations.

Pizza Da Mimmo £–££ ❽ It's not often that you need to make reservations for a low-budget pizzeria, but this place is the exception – it's excellent. It's also slightly off the beaten track: to get there, walk down Bygdøy Allé towards downtown, turn left at Nils Juels Gate, then right onto Behrens Gate. ❷ Behrens Gate 2 ❶ 22 44 40 20 ⓦ www.pizzadamimmo.no (Norwegian only) ❶ 16.00–23.00 Mon–Sat, 16.00–22.00 Sun ❷ T-bane; tram: 13, 19 to Nationaltheatret

Schillers £–££ ❾ On the site of the old Clodion Art Café, this tapas and wine bar attracts a lively crowd to sample its Spanish wines. ❷ Bygdøy Allé 63 ❶ 22 44 97 26 ❶ 16.00–23.00 Mon, 12.00–01.00 Tues–Sat, 14.00–22.00 Sun ❷ T-bane; tram: 13, 19 to Nationaltheatret

Den Gamle Majors Pub ££ ❿ A traditional pub offering light meals and an extensive drinks menu (especially beers). ❷ Bogstadveien 66 ❶ 22 46 29 04 ❶ 11.00–01.00 Mon–Sat, 12.00–01.00 Sun ❷ T-bane; tram: 11, 12, 19 to Majorstuen

Pasta Basta ££ ⓫ A decent Italian restaurant, reassuringly popular among locals. ❷ Bogstadveien 1 ❶ 22 95 53 60 ⓦ www.pasta basta.no (Norwegian only) ❶ 10.00–23.00 Mon–Sat, 12.00–23.00 Sun ❷ Tram 11, 19 to Rosenborg

△ *Majorstua is a good place to go bar-hopping*

YaYa's Restaurant ££ ⓬ Thai cuisine at its very best. A family-friendly place with great-value meals. Look for Bobo, a 360-kg (800-lb) elephant, outside the door. ⓐ Industrigata 36 ⓣ 22 83 71 10 ⓛ 16.00–22.00 Sun–Thur, 16.00–23.00 Fri & Sat (longer hours in summer) ⓝ Tram: 11, 19 to Schultz' gate

Bagatelle Restaurant £££ ⓭ Bagatelle is the only restaurant in Oslo with two Michelin stars, so be prepared to dig deep into your wallet for the gourmet food. One of Oslo's in-spots, with décor to match. ⓐ Bygdøy Allé 3 ⓣ 22 44 40 40 ⓛ 18.00–late Mon–Sat, closed Sun ⓦ www.bagatelle.no ⓝ T-bane; tram: 13, 19 to Nationaltheatret

Frognerseteren £££ ⓴ A beautiful old log building with a cosy fireplace and good views of the city, this place exudes romance. The excellent food is a further bonus. ❸ Holmenkollveien 200 ❶ 22 92 40 40 ⓦ www.frognerseteren.no ◷ 12.00–22.00 Mon–Sat, 13.00–21.00 Sun Ⓝ T-bane: Frognerseteren

Holmenkollen Restaurant £££ ⓯ Serving a mix of Norwegian and international dishes, the restaurant at the famous ski jump dates all the way back to 1892. Check out the views of Oslo and Oslofjorden. ❸ Holmenkollveien 119 ❶ 22 13 92 00 ⓦ www.holmenkollen restaurant.no (Norwegian only) ◷ 11.30–23.30 Mon–Sat, 11.30–20.00 Sun Ⓝ T-bane: Holmenkollen

hos Thea £££ ⓰ A warm and friendly restaurant with a large fireplace to give it that extra added glow. ❸ Gabels Gate 11 ❶ 22 44 68 74 ⓦ www.hosthea.no ◷ 17.00–late daily Ⓝ Tram: 13 to Skillebekk

Palace Grill £££ ⓱ You can't make a reservation for this small, hip restaurant, so expect a bit of a wait, while watching Oslo's trendies on parade. There's no à la carte menu, just a ten-course meal, so come hungry! ❸ Solligata 2 ❶ 23 13 11 40 ◷ Bar: 15.00–03.00 Mon–Sat, 15.00–01.00 Sun; restaurant: from 17.00 daily Ⓝ T-bane; tram: 13, 19 to Nationaltheatret

● *The Norwegian king's summer house in Bergen*

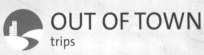

OUT OF TOWN
trips

Bergen

Norway's second city and historic capital makes for a delightful short break from Oslo. Famous for its wooden buildings at the Hanseatic wharf in old Bryggen, Bergen was once the most populous and important city in Norway. Among later claims to fame, it was the home of composer Edvard Grieg. By far the best way of reaching the city is via the Norway in a Nutshell tour (see page 118), which allows you to take in some of the country's most spectacular scenery and fjords on the way. If you're in a hurry, you can also take the train direct from Olso to Bergen – the trip takes around six and a half hours by night or seven and a half hours during the day, but it's worth going in daylight hours for the views. Either way, you'll happily spend at least a couple of days in Bergen, browsing the lively waterfront area, taking a harbour ferry, or zipping up the funicular to the top of the 320-m (1,000-ft) Mount Fløyen for a view of the city and its gorgeous surroundings. To make the most of your time, consider purchasing a Bergen Card from the tourist office (ⓐ Mathallen, Torget ⓦ www.visitbergen.com), which, among other things, gives free admission to most museums and free travel on local buses and the funicular.

SIGHTS & ATTRACTIONS

Bryggen
Designated a UNESCO World Heritage Site, Bryggen is famous for its pretty wooden buildings with pointed gables facing the harbour. The area dates back to the 14th century, when Bergen joined the Hanseatic League and became a major northern trading centre. The Bryggens Museum displays artefacts uncovered in archaeological

digs from 1955 to 1972, and also shows the foundations of the city's oldest buildings on the original site. The chance to dig came after a disastrous fire in 1955 burned many of the buildings. Excavations under the burned ruins uncovered over a million items, including proof that the area had burned many times, from as early as 1170.

Bryggens Museum ⓐ Dreggsalmenning 3 ⓣ 55 58 80 30
ⓦ www.bymuseet.no ⓛ 10.00–17.00 daily (mid-May–Aug); 11.00–15.00 Mon–Fri, 12.00–15.00 Sat, 12.00–16.00 Sun (Sept–mid-May) ⓘ Admission charge

Håkonshallen (Haakon's Hall)

This medieval castle was built by King Haakon Haakonsson in the mid-13th century, when Bergen was the political centre of Norway. The castle was badly damaged in World War II but has been extensively restored. ⓐ Bergenhus Festning ⓣ 55 31 60 67 ⓛ 10.00–16.00 daily (mid-May–Aug); 12.00–15.00 Fri–Wed, 12.00–18.00 Thur (Sept–mid-May) ⓘ Admission charge

Mariakirken (St Mary's Church)

This is the oldest building in Bergen; an outstanding Romanesque church, it was built of stone early in the 12th century. The Baroque pulpit was donated by Hanseatic merchants in 1676, and is partly made of turtle leather. It is closed for restoration until 2015. ⓐ Dreggen 15 ⓣ 55 31 59 60

Mount Fløyen & Mount Ulriken

There are wonderful panoramas to be enjoyed from the surrounding hills, which can be reached by funicular or cable car. Fløibanen is a funicular that takes you up 320 m (1,000 ft) to the top of Mount Fløyen, where you get a great view of Bergen. There are several hiking trails at the top, including one that lets you walk back down to the city. Ulriksbanen is a cable car that takes you up 640 m (2,100 ft) to the top of Mount Ulriken, where there is a café, radio

🔺 *Bergen takes its name from the hills which rise directly behind it*

NORWAY IN A NUTSHELL

You can't leave Norway without seeing some of the country's beautiful fjords – they're its most famous natural attraction for a reason. The excellent **Norway in a Nutshell** tour (ⓦ www.norwaynutshell.com) allows you to combine a trip to Bergen with a thrilling train ride, some extraordinary scenery and a visit to some of the best of Norway's western fjords.

As it leaves Oslo, the train sweeps out of the city and across the country's mountainous spine, with its forests, lakes and glaciers. The railway was completed in 1909 and is considered to be an engineering feat. It's 483 km (300 miles) long and has some 300 bridges and 200 tunnels, all of which you will journey past in around seven hours. At Myrdal, a 19.5-km (12-mile) spur line plunges down 900 m (2,800 ft) in just under an hour, to Flåm. This handy little town is really little more than a whistle stop for the train. You'll want to make a connection to Aurland, a charming country village a few kilometres north, whose speciality is *geitost* (goat's cheese). If your train ride into Flåm hasn't satisfied your need for mountain scenery, take the train to Berekvam and hike or bike the gravel road back down to Flåm. Be sure to bring a picnic.

From Flåm most 'nutshellers' catch one of the fjord cruises. Be prepared for 90 minutes of non-stop camera clicking as tourists scurry back and forth across the boat decks in quest of the perfect photo. Most boats travel along the narrow Aurlandsfjord and then up the Nærøyfjord (a UNESCO World

Heritage Site) to Gudvangen, where buses will shuttle you to the town of Voss. At Voss it's time to hop back on the train and proceed to Bergen. When you're ready to leave Bergen, simply catch the overnight train back to Oslo. The whole trip, if done non-stop, takes just 24 hours – truly, Norway in a Nutshell.

tower, hiking trails and a spectacular panoramic view of the city and surrounding fjords. In summer, sightseeing, hop-on, hop-off double-decker buses leave from Zachariasbryggen at the Fish Market to the foot of Ulriken.

Fløibanen ⊙ Vetrlidsallmenning 21 ❶ 55 33 68 00 ⓦ www.floibanen. com ⏱ 07.30–24.00 Mon–Fri, 08.00–24.00 Sat, 09.00–24.00 Sun (May–Aug); 07.30–23.00 Mon–Fri, 08.00–23.00 Sat, 09.00–23.00 Sun (Sept–Apr)

Ulriksbanen ⊙ Haukelandsbakken 40 ❶ 53 64 36 43 ⓦ www. ulriken643.no ⏱ 09.00–21.00 daily (May–Sept); 09.00–17.00 daily (Oct–Apr) ❶ Closed in bad weather

Rosenkrantztårnet (Rosenkrantz Tower)

The tower was built in the 1560s by Erik Rosenkrantz, governor of the city, and is now considered one of the finest Renaissance monuments in Norway. It served as both a residence and a fortified tower for Bergen and incorporated earlier fortifications, parts of which date back to the 1270s. In those days it was the residence of King Eirik Magnusson, the last king to hold court in Bergen, until he died in 1299. Guided tours only, every hour. ⊙ Bergenhus Festning ❶ 55 31 43 80 ⏱ 10.00–16.00 daily (mid-May–Aug); 12.00–15.00 Sun only (Sept–mid-May)

CULTURE

Bergen Kunstmuseum (Bergen Art Museum)

This museum includes work from the 15th century onwards, as well as paintings by Munch and Picasso. The adjoining Bergen Kunsthall features changing exhibitions of contemporary art. ❷ Rasmus Meyers Allé 3, 7 & 9 ❶ 55 56 80 00 ❿ www.kunstmuseene.no ❹ 11.00–17.00 daily (mid-May–mid-Sept); 11.00–17.00 Tues–Sun closed Mon (mid-Sept–mid-May) ❶ Admission charge

Bergens Sjøfartsmuseum (Bergen Maritime Museum)

Like its counterpart in Oslo (see page 96), this museum tells the story of Norwegian shipping from early times to the present day. Established in 1921, it has a huge collection of models of Viking ships and other working boats. ❷ Haakon Shetsligs Plass 15 ❶ 55 54 96 00 ❿ www.bsj.vib.no ❹ 11.00–15.00 daily

Grieghallen

Bergen's concert hall – and Norway's largest auditorium – is named after its most famous citizen, composer Edvard Grieg. The Bergen Philharmonic Orchestra (❿ www.harmonien.no), founded in 1765, performs here every Thursday evening from September to May. ❷ Edvard Griegs plass 1 ❶ 55 21 61 00 ❿ www.grieghallen.no

Hanseatiske Museum & Schøtstuene

This is one of the best-preserved wooden buildings in Bergen. Built in 1704, it is furnished to look like the home of a Hanseatic merchant in the 18th century. Schøtstuene, next to the Mariakirken, is an offshoot of the museum, comprising a collection of old Bryggen buildings. ❶ 55 54 46 90 ❿ www.museumvest.no ❶ Admission charge

Hanseatic Museum ⓐ Finnegårdsgaten 1A ⓛ 09.00–17.00 daily
(mid-May–mid-Sept); 11.00–14.00 Tues–Sat, 11.00–16.00 Sun, closed
Mon (mid-Sept–mid-May)

Schøtstuene ⓐ Øvregaten 50 ⓛ 09.00–17.00 daily (mid-May–mid-
Sept); 11.00–14.00 Sun only (mid-Sept–mid-May)

🔺 Take the Fløibanen for breathtaking views of Bergen

Den Nationale Scene (Norwegian National Theatre)

Founded in 1850 by Ole Bull, Bergen's famed violinist, the theatre is housed in a landmark Art Nouveau building. Henrik Ibsen was a director here between 1851 and 1857. ❷ Engen 1 ❶ 55 60 70 80 Ⓦ www.dns.no

Norges Fiskerimuseum (Norwegian Museum of Fisheries)

Established in 1880, this is the oldest museum of its type in Norway. Now in 'new' premises, in storehouses dating back to 1670, it displays the natural resources, management and products of the fishing industry, which is still a major element in Norway's economy. ❷ Sandriksboder 23 ❶ 55 69 96 01 Ⓦ www.museumvest.no ❶ 11.00–16.00 daily (mid-May–mid-Sept)

Universitetsmuseet Bergen (University Museum of Bergen)

The University Museum of Bergen has two departments: the Cultural History Collections (Kulturhistoriske Samlinger) and the Natural History Collections (Naturhistoriske Samlinger), as well as a botanic garden. Though parts of the collections will close at

THE HANSEATIC LEAGUE

This alliance of powerful German trading cities arose in the Middle Ages and long monopolised the profitable trade in raw materials between Scandinavia, the Baltic states and northern Europe. Its outposts reached as far as Riga and Tallinn, and Bergen was its northernmost trading station. Hanseatic merchants lived a rigid, monk-like existence, forbidden to marry or dwell outside their trading colony.

different times, the museum remains open during the extensive renovation works that are planned to finish in 2014, the year in which Norway celebrates the 200th anniversary of its constitution. One ticket gives entry to both collections.

The Cultural History Collections have several floors of exhibits, with the Viking age, Norwegian church and folk art, the history of rural communities, furniture and textiles, and Ibsen all well represented. Other, non-Norwegian, displays include Nepalese masks, Egyptian mummies and Inuit artefacts. The old zoological exhibits in the Natural History Collections are well preserved, while the geological displays bring the subject up to date with a special section on the Norwegian oil industry. You can still visit the museum's original garden, which was the university's botanic garden until 1996 when it was replaced by a new one at Milde, about 20 km (12 miles) outside the city. The old garden is small but crammed with interesting species.

Cultural History Collections ⓐ Haakon Shetligs plass 10 ⓣ 55 58 31 40
Natural History Collections ⓐ Museplass 3 ⓣ 55 58 29 20
ⓦ www.uib.no ⓛ 10.00–16.00 Tues–Fri, 11.00–16.00 Sat & Sun, closed Mon (June–Aug); 10.00–15.00 Tues–Fri, 11.00–16.00 Sat & Sun, closed Mon (Sept–May) ⓘ Admission charge
Museum Garden ⓛ 08.30–23.00 daily
Greenhouse ⓛ 10.00–12.00 & 13.00–14.30 Mon–Fri, closed Sat & Sun

USF Verftet

This former sardine factory has been converted to Bergen's main cultural centre, with a full range of contemporary arts such as music, film, dance and theatre. ⓐ Georgernes Verft ⓣ 55 30 74 10 ⓦ www.usf.no (Norwegian only)

**Vestlandske Kunstindustrimuseum
(West Norway Museum of Decorative Art)**

This museum has several permanent collections, as well as changing exhibits. The museum holds some 33,000 artworks – only a fraction of its collection is on display. Among the highlights are a collection of Bergen silver and one of the world's oldest and most beautiful violins, dating back to 1562, which was played by Norwegian virtuoso Ole Bull, the illustrious musical son of Bergen. ⓐ Nordahl Bruns Gate 9 ⓣ 55 33 66 33 ⓦ www.kunstmuseene.no ⓛ 11.00–17.00 daily (mid-May–mid-Sept); 12.00–16.00 Tues–Sun, closed Mon (mid-Sept–mid-May) ⓘ Admission charge

RETAIL THERAPY

A trading centre for centuries, Bergen continues the tradition today, with everything from small specialist shops to large malls.

Audhild Viken began production more than 60 years ago. Over the decades it began offering other crafts and souvenirs, winning awards from the Norwegian Design Council along the way. Today you can find a wide range of Norwegian goods including slippers and gloves, underwear, trolls, jackets, jumpers and sheepskin. ⓐ Bellgården ⓣ 55 21 54 89 ⓦ www.gifts.no ⓛ 09.00–22.30 daily (mid-June–Aug); 10.00–17.00 Mon–Fri, 10.00–16.00 Sat, closed Sun (Sept–mid-June)

Bergen Steinsenter Jewellery, watches, and objects made of stone and minerals are the draw here. A good place to find an original ornament or gift. ⓐ Bredsgården Bryggen ⓣ 55 32 82 60 ⓦ www. steinsenter.no ⓛ 11.00–17.00 Mon–Sat, closed Sun (summer); 11.00–15.00 Tues–Sat, closed Sun & Mon (winter)

Bergen Storsenter Home to more than 70 stores, this is the biggest shopping centre in Bergen. Services include a pharmacy and a dentist.
ⓐ Stromgaten 8 **ⓣ** 55 21 24 60 **ⓛ** 09.00–21.00 Mon–Fri, 09.00–18.00 Sat, closed Sun

🔺 *Bryggen carries on Bergen's centuries-old commercial traditions*

Bryggen Husflid A/S This sweater specialist carries handknits and a wide range of brands, including Dale of Norway and Gjestal. It's also a popular choice for souvenirs such as woodcarvings and trolls. ⓐ Bugården Bryggen ⓣ 55 32 88 03 ⓦ www.sweaterspecialist.com ⓛ Times vary

Elg A small shop specialising in moose of varying sizes, shapes and materials. ⓐ Bryggen 11 ⓣ 55 21 54 88 ⓦ www.gifts.no ⓛ 11.00–18.00 Mon–Sat, closed Sun

Galleriet This shopping mall with over 70 outlets caters to most needs. Clothes, books, cafés, a pharmacy, souvenirs and art galleries are all here. ⓐ Torgallmenningen 8 ⓣ 55 30 05 00 ⓦ www.galleriet.com ⓛ 09.00–21.00 Mon–Fri, 09.00–18.00 Sat, closed Sun

Glass Thomsen A specialist in glass, crystal, dinner sets and gift articles. They have skilled staff and good service. ⓐ Kløverhuset shopping centre (see below) ⓣ 55 33 03 11 ⓛ 09.00–20.00 Mon–Fri, 09.00–18.00 Sat, closed Sun

Julehuset The Christmas Shop is a year-round stop-off for a yule-related gift or decoration. Don't miss the large selection of typical *nisser* (Norwegian Santa Clauses). ⓐ Holmedalsgården 1 ⓣ 55 21 51 00 ⓛ 09.00–22.00 Mon–Sat, 10.00–21.00 Sun (shorter hours in winter)

Kløverhuset Norway's oldest shopping centre stocks the latest fashions, with the emphasis on upmarket and trendy lines. ⓐ Strandgaten 13–15 ⓣ 55 31 37 90 ⓛ 10.00–20.00 Mon–Fri, 10.00–18.00 Sat, closed Sun

Nilssen på Bryggen Conveniently located along the wharf, Nilssen på Bryggen focuses on all things woollen, with a wide range of knitwear and embroidery. ❷ Bryggen 3 ❶ 55 31 67 90 ❸ 09.00–20.00 Mon–Fri, 09.00–18.00 Sat, 10.00–18.00 Sun (June–Aug); 09.00–16.30 Mon–Wed & Fri, 09.00–19.00 Thur, 09.00–15.00 Sat, closed Sun (Sept–May)

Ruben's Skattkammer For a bit of fun, check out this toy and game store. Educational materials also feature, while costumes and souvenirs round out the stock. ❷ Vetrlidsalmenning 5 ❶ 55 31 41 11 ❸ 09.30–17.00 Mon–Wed, Fri & Sat, 09.30–18.00 Thur, closed Sun

TAKING A BREAK

Baker Brun £ Don't leave Bergen without trying a *skillingsbolle* (cinnamon bun) from this little bakery at Bryggen.
❷ Damsgårdsvei 109A ❶ 55 31 65 12 ❸ 07.00–21.00 daily (June–Aug); 07.00–17.00 daily (Sept–May)

Dr Livingstone Travellers Café £ As the name hints, this place features a menu of foods from around the globe. The outdoor seating area is nice in warm weather. Great coffee bar, too.
❷ Kong Oscarsgate 12 ❶ 55 56 03 12 ❸ 16.00–23.00 Tues–Sat, closed Sun

Søstrene Hagelin £ This seafood place opened in 1929 and, after a couple of moves, is still going today. Be sure to try the fish soup. You can eat in or take away for a picnic. ❷ Strandgaten 3 ❶ 55 90 20 13
❸ 09.00–19.00 Mon–Fri, 10.00–17.00 Sat, closed Sun

Beredt Kløver Cafè £–££ Sit on the top floor of Kløverhuset (see page 126) and take in the view while enjoying traditional Norwegian dishes or coffee and cakes at reasonable prices. ❷ Strandgaten 13–15 ❶ 55 62 54 58 ❸ 10.00–20.00 Mon–Fri, 10.00–18.00 Sat, closed Sun

Det Lille Kaffekompaniet £–££ A tiny bar serving good coffee and delicious cake and ice cream. ❷ Nedre Fjellsmauet 2 ❶ 55 32 92 72 ❸ 10.00–22.00 Sun–Fri, 10.00–18.00 Sat

Kafe Kippers USF ££ This café at the popular arts venue is a gathering spot for local artists and arty types. The Friday live jazz sessions are renowned. The on-site outdoor restaurant, Kaien, is one of Bergen's largest, with a view of the city fjord. ❷ Georgenes Verft 3 ❶ 55 30 40 80 ❿ www.usf.no (Norwegian only) ❸ 11.00–23.00 Mon–Thur, 11.00–24.00 Fri, 12.00–24.00 Sat, 12.00–23.00 Sun

Hanne på Høyden £££ A bit on the pricey side, but it's worth paying the bill in order to enjoy a fine menu of seasonal Norwegian food at its very best. ❷ Fosswinckelsgate 18 ❶ 55 32 34 32 ❸ 11.30–22.00 Mon–Sat, closed Sun

AFTER DARK

RESTAURANTS
Bryggens Tracteursted £££ One of several good restaurants at Bryggen, this place offers a modern twist on traditional Norwegian food with an open-air backyard in summer. ❷ Bryggestredet 2 ❶ 55 33 69 99 ❿ www.bellevue.no ❸ 11.00–22.00 daily (summer); 17.00–22.00 Tues–Sat, closed Sun & Mon (winter)

Fløien Folkerestaurant £££ Originally opened in 1925, this summer-only restaurant at the top of Mount Fløyen offers an extensive menu and amazing views – book well in advance and request a window seat. There's also a cheaper café, open all day in summer and at weekends in the winter months. ⓐ Fløyfjellet 2 ⓣ 55 32 18 75 ⓦ www.bellevue.no ⓛ Restaurant: 17.00–22.00 daily (May–Sept); café: 10.00–22.00 daily (May–Sept); 12.00–17.00 Fri–Sun only (Oct–Apr)

BARS & CLUBS

Fotballpuben Probably the most popular football pub in Bergen. Especially lively on nights when the local team, Brann, is playing. Downstairs is the late-night club. ⓐ Vestre Torggaten 9 ⓣ 55 33 66 61 ⓦ www.fotballpuben.no ⓛ 09.00–03.00 Mon–Sat, 12.00–03.00 Sun

Garage Bergen's number one rock club caters to a twenty- and thirty-something crowd. ⓐ Christies Gate 14 ⓣ 55 32 19 80

⬤ Nightfall in Bergen, with its many bars and clubs

◆ *Bergen city from the top of Mount Fløyen*

Ⓦ www.garage.no (Norwegian only) 🕒 15.00–03.00 Mon–Sat, 17.00–03.00 Sun

Hulen Rockclub Not your average club: this one is situated in a cave. ⓐ Olaf Ryes vei 47 ⓣ 55 33 38 30 Ⓦ www.hulen.no (Norwegian only) 🕒 21.00–03.00 Wed–Sat, closed Sun–Tues

Metro The place to come if you want to dance to the latest hits. Remember to dress up. ⓐ Nedre Ole Bulls Plass 4 ⓣ 55 90 19 60 Ⓦ www.metronightclub.no 🕒 22.00–02.30 Sun–Thur, 22.00–03.00 Fri & Sat

Rick's Café og Salonger Drinking and dancing are the attractions at this large club, whose different areas host quiz and comedy nights, a lounge bar, DJ nights and live bands. ⓐ Øvre Ole Bulls Plass 9 ⓣ 55 55 31 31 Ⓦ www.ricks.no (Norwegian only) 🕒 16.00–03.00 daily, times vary

The Scotsman A two-storey establishment with a piano bar in the basement. Live football matches are shown here. ⓐ Valkendorfsgate 1B ⓣ 55 21 80 00 🕒 15.00–03.00 daily

Wessel Pub For decades this has been one of the most popular pubs in Bergen. Informal and packed and offering a wide range of aquavits. ➋ Øvre Ole Bulls Plass 6 ➊ 55 55 49 54 ➍ www.wesselbar.no ➌ 15.00–00.30 Mon–Thur, 15.00–01.30 Fri, 12.00–01.30 Sat, 16.00–00.30 Sun

ACCOMMODATION

Augustin Hotel £££–£££ Bergen's oldest family-run hotel integrates modern amenities with good old-fashioned service. Rooms are comfortable, and some have harbour views. ➋ C Sundtsgate 22–24 ➊ 55 30 40 00 ➍ www.augustin.no

Comfort Hotel Holberg ££–£££ This well-located hotel, with a rooftop terrace, is named after 18th-century poet Ludvig Holberg, who was born in a house on the site. It also boasts a health club with sauna, steam bath and solarium. ➋ Strandgaten 190 ➊ 55 30 42 07 ➍ www.choice.no

Best Western Hotel Hordaheimen £££ In the heart of the city, very close to the railway station, this is one of Bergen's most venerable hotels, though it was renovated in 2011. ➋ C Sundtsgate 18 ➊ 55 33 50 00 ➍ www.bestwestern.com

Scandic Bergen City £££ A modern conference-style hotel with large and comfortable rooms. ➋ Håkonsgaten 2–7 ➊ 55 30 90 80 ➍ www.scandic-hotels.no

Thon Hotel Rosenkrantz £££ A traditional hotel with excellent service. ➋ Rosenkrantz Gate 7 ➊ 55 30 14 00 ➍ www.thonhotels.com

Hurtigruten tours

Everyone's image of Norway focuses on the fjords that slice deeply into its western shore, creating one of the world's most spectacular coastlines. Options range from a six-day cruise from Kirkenes to Bergen, to packages combining boat, train and bus travel, to trips with a special theme, like a whale safari or search for the Northern Lights. From September to April the Northern Lights perform brilliant shows in the dark sky, although daylight hours are very short: from mid-November to mid-January in the far north the sun never rises.

Beautiful fjord scenery is just one reason for taking the legendary coastal voyage on one of the 14 ships of Norway's Hurtigruten line. The name translates as 'fast route' and these ships were once the only connection between Norway's northern coastal towns. Today's modern vessels still provide vital local transport, but are also popular for their views: from almost any place on the ships passengers can watch the changing panorama of mountains, islands, fjords and little fishing harbours. For an outline of the route, see the map on page 115.

While day passengers can use the ships to take them to remote coastal towns and islands, many travellers take the entire route, either from Bergen to Kirkenes or vice versa. Some make the trip both ways, because the ship makes daytime stops on the southbound trip where it stopped at night on the way north. An added attraction is a visit to the stunning Geirangerfjord on summer northbound sailings. Optional excursions are reasonably priced, often leaving the ship at one stop and travelling overland to re-board at a later port. Especially worthwhile are those to the North Cape, Vesterålen and Lofoten.

Port stops vary from 15 minutes to several hours. In Vardø passengers follow a costumed drummer to the octagonal Vardohus

Fort, built in the 1700s, for sea views and tours of the fort's historic buildings. In Stokmarknes the Hurtigruten Museum recalls the service's founding here in 1893. Ålesund, where the ship stops at night on its southern voyage, is worth staying up for. Its Art Nouveau centre is floodlit and only a short walk from the dock. One of the attractions of the Norwegian Coastal Voyage is its flexibility. The ships sail all year, departing every day. Options range from cruise-only six-day trips from Kirkenes to Bergen, to 17-day packages that combine a 12-day return-trip with days to explore Bergen and Oslo. Schedules and bookings can be made via 🔃 www.hurtigruten.com

◯ *Stop at beautiful Trondheim on your way to the northern fjords*

SIGHTS & ATTRACTIONS

Hammerfest

This small city was levelled in World War II, when it was the headquarters for the German fleet in the North Atlantic. The crypt of Hammerfest Church was the only structure to survive, and one entire end wall of the striking rebuilt church is now a stained-glass window. A museum of the reconstruction, Gjenreisningsmuseet, explores the forced evacuation of Hammerfest and the Germans' 'scorched earth' policy in the region during World War II, as well as the town's struggle to rebuild its homes and community after the war. The Royal & Ancient Polar Bear Society is a favourite stop for its small displays recording Hammerfest's relationship with this Arctic creature as well as its history since the 1600s as a centre for traders from Russia, the Arctic and as far away as southern Europe. You can become a member, earning the right to wear the club emblem.

Gjenreisningsmuseet ⓐ Kirkegata 21 ⓣ 78 40 29 40
ⓦ www.kystmuseene.no ⓛ 09.00–16.00 Mon–Fri, 10.00–14.00
Sat & Sun (June–mid-Aug); 11.00–14.00 daily (mid-Aug–June)
ⓘ Admission charge, free Dec–Jan

Royal & Ancient Polar Bear Society ⓐ Harnegata 3 ⓣ 78 41 21 85
ⓛ 09.00–16.00 Mon–Fri, 10.00–14.00 Sat & Sun (Aug–May);
06.00–18.00 Mon–Fri, 06.00–16.00 Sat & Sun (June & July)

Harstad, Vesterålen

Hurtigruten passengers on the Coastal Express can opt for a shore excursion to explore the scenic Vesterålen region by land. In Harstad, you'll find the medieval Trondenes Church. Its unusual rood screen holds a painted pulpit, and the three altars have polychrome, carved wooden statues. Also worth a visit is the Trondenes District Museum, telling the story of the area from the Viking period and Middle Ages to World War II, with signage in English. Recent history is even more vividly told on a hill above town, where in a completely restored fortification is the enormous Adolf Gun, the world's largest land-based gun, built by the Germans in World War II. The small islands, connected by ferries, form a major agricultural area famed for its delicious strawberries, which ripen in August.

Vesterålen Reiseliv (Tourist Office) ❸ Kjøpmannsgata 2, Sortland ❶ 76 11 14 80 ❼ www.visitvesteralen.com

Trondenes District Museum ❸ Harstad ❶ 77 01 83 80 ❹ 10.00–17.00 daily (mid-June–mid-Aug); 10.00–14.00 Mon–Fri, 11.00–16.00 Sun, closed Sat (mid-Aug–mid-June)

North Cape

Europe's northernmost point is more than a geographical landmark. The continent ends here in a sheer drop into jagged rocks and crashing waves. Fog frequently envelops the cape, and in the early summer mornings the sun plays with fog to create a constantly changing land- and seascape. The glass-enclosed Nordkapphallen (North Cape Hall) has exhibits describing local wildlife and the story of the World War II Battle of North Cape. If you have a taste for champagne, then visit the world's northernmost champagne bar.

Nordkapphallen ❸ Honningsvåg ❶ 78 47 68 60 ❼ www.visitnorth cape.no ❹ 11.00–01.00 daily (mid-May–mid-Aug); 11.00–22.00 daily (mid–end Aug); 11.00–15.00 daily (Sept); advance booking only in winter ❶ Admission charge

Tromsø

Walk straight up the hill from the harbour to reach the busy main street, Storgata, which is kept lively by the city's large student population. Almost untouched by World War II, Tromsø retains the largest collection of 19th-century wooden buildings north of Trondheim. Look out in particular for the group known as Skansen, near the harbour.

There are plenty of other sights in Tromsø. The Polar Museum in the heart of the old town is a preserved 1830s customs building housing low-tech exhibits on polar exploration. Polaria is a multi-faceted discovery centre: learning experiences centre around polar regions, with films, sea aquarium, live seals and polar research exhibits. The Arctic Botanical Garden, open 24 hours a day, year-round, is a good free introduction to the flora of this harsh region. Visitors interested in local Sami, prehistoric and Viking culture, as well as the nature and history of northern Norway, should spend an hour or two at the outstanding University Museum. It includes some of the many ancient rock carvings found nearby, and the Viking area has a full-sized replica Viking longhouse. Finally, to appreciate the city's splendid setting between the mountains and sea, ride the Fjellheisen cable car up to Storsteinen, 380 m (1,200 ft) above.

Tourist Office ❸ Kirkegata 2 ❶ 77 61 00 00 Ⓦ www.visittromso.no Ⓛ 09.00–16.00 Mon–Fri, 10.00–16.00 Sat, closed Sun (Sept–mid-May); 09.00–19.00 Mon–Fri, 10.00–17.00 Sat & Sun (mid-May–Aug)

Arktisk-alpin Botanisk hage (Arctic Botanical Gardens) Ⓝ Bus: 20 to the university in Breivika

Fjellheisen cable car ❸ Solleveien 12 ❶ 77 63 87 37 Ⓛ 10.00–01.00 daily (mid-May–early Aug); 10.00–22.00 daily (early–late Aug), 10.00–17.00 daily (Sept); 11.00–16.00 daily (Oct–mid-Apr); 10.00–17.00 daily (mid-Apr–mid-May)

Polaria ❸ Hjalmar Johansensgate 12 ❶ 77 75 01 00 Ⓦ www.polaria.no Ⓛ 10.00–19.00 daily (mid-May–mid-Aug); 12.00–17.00 daily (mid-Aug–mid-May)

Polar Museum ⓐ Søndre Tollbugate 11 ⓣ 77 60 66 30 ⓦ www.polar museum.no ⓛ 10.00–19.00 daily (mid-June–mid-Aug); 11.00–17.00 daily (mid-Aug–Sept & Mar–mid-June); 11.00–16.00 daily (Oct–Feb)

Universitetsmuseet Tromsø (Tromsø University Museum)
ⓐ Lars Thørings Veg 10 ⓣ 77 64 50 00 ⓦ www.uit.no ⓛ 09.00–18.00 daily (June–Aug); 10.00–16.30 Mon–Fri, 12.00–15.00 Sat, 11.00–16.00 Sun (Sept–May) ⓘ Admission charge

Trondheim

The main attractions of Trondheim are the beautiful Nidaros Cathedral and the streets lined with old houses. The earliest parts of the cathedral date from the 11th century, and the statues in the façade date from the Middle Ages to the 1980s. Highlights include the magnificent organ in the north transept and the St Olaf altar front (1300). The world's first bicycle lift, to Kristiansten Fort, is near Gamle Bybro, the picturesque 1618 bridge. Among the historic buildings at Trøndelag Folk Museum is a stave church from 1170.

Trondheim Activum (Tourist Office) ⓐ Torget ⓣ 73 80 76 60
ⓦ www.visit-trondheim.com ⓛ 09.00–16.00 Mon–Fri, 10.00–14.00 Sat, closed Sun (winter – longer hours in summer)

Trøndelage Folkemuseum (Trøndelag Folk Museum) ⓐ Sverresborg Allé 13 ⓣ 73 89 01 10 ⓦ www.sverresborg.no ⓛ 11.00–18.00 daily (June–Aug); 11.00–15.00 Mon–Fri, 12.00–16.00 Sat & Sun (Sept–May)

RETAIL THERAPY

Blåst Glasshytta Visit this glassblowing workshop to see beautiful glassware being made. ⓐ Hansensgate 4, Tromsø ⓣ 77 68 34 60
ⓛ 10.00–17.00 Mon–Fri, 10.00–15.00 Sat, closed Sun

Galleri Nordnorge The local artists' association operates this permanent gallery of the Festival of North Norway. Along with paintings and drawings are fine crafts. ⓐ Normannsgata 1A, Harstad ⓣ 77 02 81 00 ⓛ 12.00–15.00 Fri–Sun

Gjenreisningsmuseet This museum shop sells crafts, including handmade candles, along with books and souvenirs. ⓐ Kirkegata 21, Hammerfest ⓣ 78 40 29 30 ⓛ See page 134

Perlehuset For creative souls this shop is worth a visit. Buy beads and pearls in any shape and colour to create your own jewellery. ⓐ Jomfrugata 14, Trondheim ⓣ 73 52 43 49 ⓦ www.perlehuset-trondheim.no ⓛ 10.00–17.00 Mon–Wed & Fri, 10.00–18.00 Thur, 10.00–16.00 Sat, closed Sun

Royal & Ancient Polar Bear Society The little gift shop is the perfect place to buy furry white toy bears for kids, as well as books and souvenirs relating to the Arctic and polar bears. ⓐ Havnegata 3, Hammerfest ⓣ 78 41 31 00 ⓦ www.isbjorn klubben.no ⓛ 06.00–18.00 Mon–Fri, 06.00–16.00 Sat & Sun (June & July); 09.00–16.00 Mon–Fri, 10.00–14.00 Sat & Sun (Aug–May)

TAKING A BREAK

Gjenreisningsmuseet Cafeteria £ Freshly made waffles, coffee, hot chocolate and cakes are served in the Reconstruction Museum's neat little café. ⓐ Kirkegata 21, Hammerfest ⓣ 78 40 29 30 ⓛ 09.00–16.00 Mon–Fri, 10.00–14.00 Sat & Sun (June–mid-Aug); 11.00–14.00 daily (mid-Aug–May)

Kaffistova £ Home-style Norwegian cooking in a casual restaurant-café. It's 100 years old and is Harstad's oldest café. ➋ Rik Kaarbøsgate 6, Harstad ➊ 77 06 12 57 ➍ 08.00–18.00 Mon–Fri, 09.00–15.30 Sat, 12.00–17.00 Sun

Mormors stue £–££ A friendly café with an old-fashioned interior. ➋ Nedre Enkeltskillingveita 2, Trondheim ➊ 73 52 20 22 Ⓦ www. mormor.no (Norwegian only) ➍ 10.00–23.30 Mon–Sat, 13.00–23.30 Sun

AFTER DARK

Look to swinging Tromsø for nightlife, although its nickname 'the Paris of the North' may be an exaggeration. Storgata is where the action is – and you can forget dress codes: the small coastal town's nightlife is mostly low-key. In terms of cuisine, you might see some unusual menu choices, such as seaweed, seagull eggs and seal lasagne! With its large student population, Trondheim has a busy nightlife, with numerous bars, pubs and clubs; the area around Nordregate is a good starting point here. If you want a quiet night in the pub or a meal of freshly caught fish, the fishing village of Honningsvåg is a good choice.

RESTAURANTS

Ørens Kro ££–£££ This 1863 tavern keeps its cosy old-time atmosphere, while being a popular meeting place for young professionals who work in the riverside neighbourhood. Drinks, light dishes and an à la carte dinner menu. ➋ Dokkgata 8, Trondheim ➊ 73 60 06 35 ➍ 15.30–01.00 Mon–Sat, closed Sun

Restaurant Kompasset ££–£££ Traditional Norwegian dishes using, where possible, locally produced ingredients. ⓐ North Cape Hall, Honningsvåg ⓣ 78 47 68 60 ⓛ 11.00–01.00 daily (mid-May–Aug only) ⓘ Advance booking essential

Emma's Drømmekjøkken £££ 'The kitchen of Emma's dreams', as this restaurant is called, serves tasty meat and fish dishes. Slightly pricey. ⓐ Kirkegata 8, Tromsø ⓣ 77 63 77 30 ⓦ www.emmas drommekjokken.no (Norwegian only) ⓛ 18.00–late Mon–Sat, closed Sun

BARS AND CLUBS

Downtown Trondheim's largest nightclub, with four different bar and club concepts in one. Expect long queues, especially on Thursdays and Saturdays. ⓐ Nordregate 28, Trondheim ⓣ 73 50 40 00 ⓦ www.downtown.no ⓛ 22.00–02.30 Mon–Sat, closed Sun

Rica Grand Hotel Proudly boasting that its Grand Bar is the only nightspot in Tromsø where die-hard smokers can indulge their vice in a heated area protected from the Balsfjord wind, this long-established cocktail bar has a retro theme, majoring in all the 1980s favourites. In the same hotel, Gründer is a new bar-restaurant which livens up its evenings with DJs for a party atmosphere. ⓐ Storgaten 44, Tromsø ⓣ 77 75 37 77 ⓛ Grand Bar: 19.00–02.00 Wed, Thur & Sun, 19.00–03.00 Fri & Sat, closed Mon & Tues; Gründer: 10.00–01.30 Sun–Thur, 10.00–03.00 Fri & Sat

▶ *A reminder of Viking ships on Bygdøy's waterfront*

PRACTICAL
information

Directory

GETTING THERE

By air

Several airlines offer flights to Oslo International Airport at Gardermoen (see page 50). From London Heathrow, SAS and BA have frequent services, while London Gatwick is served by Norwegian, as is Edinburgh and Manchester. SAS also flies direct to Manchester. Dubliners have a choice of SAS or Norwegian to the airport. Ryanair mainly uses Rygge International Airport south of the city, flying in from Newcastle, Manchester, Liverpool, London Gatwick and London Stansted, but it has some flights into Sandefjord Torp from Edinburgh, Liverpool and London Stansted.

SAS Ⓦ www.sas.no

British Airways Ⓦ www.ba.com

Norwegian Air Shuttle Ⓦ www.norwegian.no

Ryanair Ⓦ www.ryanair.com

Many people are aware that air travel emits CO_2, which contributes to climate change. You may be interested in the possibility of lessening the environmental impact of your flight through the charity **Climate Care** (Ⓦ www.climatecare.org), which offsets your CO_2 by funding environmental projects around the world.

By road

Oslo can be reached by car by using Highway E18 from the east or west, or Highway E6 from the north or south. With the opening of the Øresund bridge between Sweden and Denmark, it is now possible to reach Norway from the Channel ports without using a ferry. The roads in Norway are generally in good condition and well maintained, especially those in and around Oslo. If travelling in winter, always check the road conditions. The wearing of seat belts is mandatory, as is the use of headlights at all times of day. Children 12 years and younger must ride in the rear seat. Driving under the influence of alcohol is not tolerated, with the legal limit being 0.02 per cent; prison sentences and large fines are common.

The minimum age for driving is 18 years, and drivers must have a full national driving licence or an International Driving Permit (IDP). Vehicles entering Norway must have proof of registration and proof of insurance. Speed limits on highways are 80–100 kph (50–60 mph), in cities 50 kph (30 mph), with some residential areas 30 kph (18 mph). Speed limits are rigorously enforced, speed traps are abundant and the fines are high, so watch your speed.

By rail

All international trains arrive at and depart from Oslo S. A direct journey from the UK by rail will involve a cross-Channel ferry or the Eurostar to Brussels as the first leg of the journey. From London (St Pancras International) to Oslo S takes 24–30 hours, via Brussels, Cologne, Hamburg, Copenhagen and Malmö or, with fewer changes of train, via Brussels, Cologne, Copenhagen and Göteborg (Gothenburg). The monthly *Thomas Cook European Rail Timetable* has up-to-date schedules for international train services to Oslo and many Norwegian domestic routes.

Eurostar Reservations (UK) ℹ (UK) 08432 186 186 ⓦ www.eurostar.com
Thomas Cook European Rail Timetable ℹ (UK) 01733 416477; (USA) 1 800 322 3834 ⓦ www.thomascookpublishing.com

ENTRY FORMALITIES

Citizens from the EU and most English-speaking countries can visit Norway for up to three months without a visa. If arriving by car, drivers must have a national driving licence, or an International Driving Permit (see page 143). Licences must be carried at all times, as well as car registration documents and proof of valid insurance.

MONEY

Norway is not a member of the EU and has kept its traditional currency, the Norwegian krone (Kr, usually shown in foreign exchange listings as NOK). The krone is made up of 100 øre. Some shops, especially in the tourist areas, may take euros and US dollars, but this is not common practice. Banks, ATMs and currency exchange kiosks are found throughout Oslo. Major credit cards are honoured at most shops and restaurants, as are euro, US dollar and UK sterling traveller's cheques.

HEALTH, SAFETY & CRIME

By international standards, Norway is a very healthy and safe country. The July 2011 attacks were extremely atypical, the work of a lone terrorist, and have caused much soul-searching among the country's small population. Health standards are high; the water is safe to drink and the food safe to eat, although you might want to stay clear of *lutefisk* (see page 26). The biggest health concerns are flu and colds in winter, and sunburn and insect bites in summer. If you plan on hiking in the great outdoors, it would be wise to be vaccinated against tick-borne encephalitis.

Norway is a member of the European Economic Agreement, and thus has free reciprocal health agreements with all EU countries. Those that qualify need to carry their EHIC card (Ⓦ www.ehic.org.uk). The Norwegian Health Plan does not cover other nationals, but some countries' plans may cover all or part of medical costs in Norway, so visitors should check on this before departing. The costs of health care in Norway are quite reasonable compared to other Western countries, but non-EU visitors should carry adequate travel health insurance, and it is recommended even for EU visitors.

Local pharmacies and medical centres can give advice and sell medications for most minor ailments. The majority of medical professionals in Norway speak good English.

The crime rate in Oslo is low, and it is considered one of the safest capital cities in the world. However, normal precautions should be taken to avoid pickpockets, purse snatchers and other petty criminals. Oslo has a growing drug problem, and you should beware of addicts, drunks and beggars. Police officers are easily identified by their black boots and trousers (trousers have a chequered trim), light blue shirts, and black caps with a police crest. Police cars and police stations are clearly marked POLITI. The police are normally unarmed, and are very friendly, helpful and courteous, so do not hesitate to ask them for information or directions. Cars should be locked and parked in open or well-lit areas, with any valuables such as jewellery, cameras, mobile phones and computers locked in the boot or otherwise out of sight.

OPENING HOURS

Banks are open Monday–Friday, usually 08.15–15.00, except Thursday, when they stay open until 17.00. Most shops operate 09.00–17.00 Monday–Friday, closing at around 15.00 on Saturdays and only opening on Sundays during the holiday season. Supermarket hours are 09.00–21.00, except Saturday, when they close at 18.00. Restaurants generally open for breakfast (where served) 08.00–11.00, for lunch 12.00–15.00 and for dinner 18.00–23.00. Most museums open at 11.00 and close at 17.00, unless otherwise stated in this book. Some open earlier in the day, especially in summer.

TOILETS

Norway has Western-style toilets. Public toilets can be found at
shopping malls, railway stations and bus stations, but in most cases
you will have to pay up to 10Kr to use them. A few restaurants still
charge to use the facilities, although most do not. Toilets at libraries
and museums are normally free.

CHILDREN

Travelling with kids in Norway is quite easy. Many restaurants offer
children's menus, with lower prices, hotels take a kindly attitude to
travelling families, and there are plenty of sights that kids will love.
Don't miss the International Museum of Children's Art (see page
104), which houses children's art from 180 countries. Holmenkollen
(see page 102) is another favourite with young visitors. The
Norwegian Folk Museum (see page 94) is Norway's largest open-air
museum, with more than 150 buildings from all around the country.
If you book in advance, the museum will also arrange Norwegian
evenings of folk tales and folk dancing. And of course, no family
visit to Oslo would be complete without a trip to Akershus Castle
(see page 62), with its dungeons and banquet rooms. There's even a
drawbridge at the entrance.

When the weather's hot, head for the beach. The Bygdøy
Peninsula (see page 90) has two popular beaches, Huk and
Paradisbukta, which can be easily reached by bus. Another good
day trip is TusenFryd, an amusement park about 20 km (12 miles)
south of Oslo on Highway E6. It has rides, including carousels and
roller coasters, as well as swimming and a fantasy farm. The TusenFryd
bus has frequent departures from the bus station and other stops.

If you're in town on Constitution Day, 17 May, you're in luck.
Though not exactly a holiday specifically for children, it comes close.

It's dedicated to families and children, and in Oslo it's celebrated with a Children's Parade and light-hearted, family-oriented activities.

COMMUNICATIONS
Internet

There are lots of Internet cafés in Oslo, including Arctic Internet at the main railway station (☎ 22 17 19 40), which also has scanning and printing facilities. Some libraries also have access: **Deichmanske Bibliotek** (Municipal Library ⓐ Arne Garborgs Plass 4 ☎ 23 43 29 00) offers 30 minutes of free access; however, you will need to call to reserve a time. Along with its branches, it also provides free Wi-Fi.

Phone

The telephone system in Norway is very good, and quite extensive. Norway uses eight-digit numbers with no area codes. Long-distance rates in Norway are among the lowest in the world. Local calls from hotel rooms and pay phones cost 5Kr. Newsstands, post offices and railway stations sell telephone cards (TeleKort). Some payphones accept credit cards. Faxes can be sent or received from most major hotels, although it is much cheaper to send them from a post office.

900/1800 MHz mobile phones will work in Norway. Norwegian SIM cards are available, but the instructions are in Norwegian, so you might want to purchase the card directly from **Telehuset** (ⓦ www.telehuset.no), who will connect you when you buy it. Cards are also available at 7-Eleven stores and some Narvesen kiosks. Cards start at 200Kr, with 100Kr worth of calls.

Post

The postal service in Norway is very good. Mail going to other parts of Europe takes two to three days, to North America about a week.

TELEPHONING NORWAY

To call Norway, dial your home country's international exit code (usually 00), then Norway's country code, 47, plus the eight-digit local number your require. There are no area codes.

TELEPHONING ABROAD

To make an international phone call from Norway, dial 00, followed by the country's international calling code, followed by the area code (usually omitting the first 'o' if there is one) and the local number you require. Country codes include: UK 44, Republic of Ireland 353, USA and Canada 1, Australia 61, New Zealand 64 and South Africa 27.

Postage for letters and postcards to other parts of Europe costs about 12Kr, and to the rest of the world about 13Kr. Post offices normally open 09.00–17.00 weekdays, 09.00–13.00 Saturdays; some offices in Oslo stay open longer. Norway also has small post offices inside grocery shops.

ELECTRICITY

Norway uses 220 V, 50 Hz alternating current. Sockets take the standard continental plug with two round prongs. British visitors will need a plug adaptor for appliances; other visitors, including those from the US, will also need a transformer for the different voltage. Both items are best purchased at home before travelling.

SMOKING REGULATIONS

Restrictive anti-smoking laws have been in force in Norway since June 2004. In general, smoking is not allowed in any public place or on any public transport. Smoking is not allowed in restaurants, bars and pubs, even in outdoor areas if they face other public places. Many hotel rooms are now designated as non-smoking.

TRAVELLERS WITH DISABILITIES
Norway caters for travellers with disabilities better than most countries, and all new buildings are required to have wheelchair access. Most street crossings have ramps or low curbs, and crossing signals also produce audible sounds (long beeps mean that it's safe to cross, and short beeps indicate that the signal is about to change). Many trains have spaces for wheelchairs. If you travel with a wheelchair, have it serviced before your departure and carry any essentials you may need for repairs. It is also a good idea to travel with any spares of special clothing or equipment that might be difficult to replace.

However, Oslo can still be a challenge for travellers with disabilities. The Norwegian Association for the Disabled is a good source of information on hotels, restaurants and tourist attractions that are equipped to receive disabled visitors. Tourist offices also can be especially helpful in determining if there is suitable accommodation in the area you wish to visit as long as you make your request in advance.

It's a good idea to double-check any information you receive, as some establishments will advertise services that are still to be implemented. Associations dealing with your particular disability can be excellent sources of information on conditions and circumstances in other countries. The following contacts may be helpful:
Access-able Travel Source Ⓦ www.access-able.com

Australian Council for Rehabilitation of the Disabled (ACROD)
🅐 33 Thesiger Court, Deakin ACT 2600 🅣 02 6283 3200
🆆 www.nds.org.au
Disabled Persons Assembly (DPA) 🅐 4/173–175 Victoria Street,
Wellington, New Zealand 🅣 64 4 801 9100 🆆 www.dpa.org.nz
Irish Wheelchair Association 🅐 Blackheath Drive, Clontarf, Dublin 3
🅣 01 818 6400 🆆 www.iwa.ie
Norwegian Association for the Disabled 🅐 Schweigaardsgate 12,
Oslo 🅣 24 10 24 00 🆆 www.nhf.no
RADAR 🅐 12 City Forum, 250 City Road, London EC1V 8AF 🅣 020 7250
3222 🆆 www.radar.org.uk
Society for Accessible Travel & Hospitality (SATH) 🅐 347 5th Avenue,
New York, NY 10016, USA 🅣 212 447 7284 🆆 www.sath.org

TOURIST INFORMATION

The Oslo Tourist Office has three information points as well as
a call centre in Oslo. They sell Oslo Passes and can arrange
accommodation. One is near Rådhuset (this office also offers free
Wi-Fi). 🅐 Fridtjof Nansens plass 5 🅛 09.00–16.00 Mon–Fri, closed
Sat & Sun (Oct–Mar); 09.00–17.00 daily (Apr–Sept). Another office,
which has the longest opening hours and is open 365 days a year,
is by Oslo Central Station. 🅐 Jernbanetorget 1 🅛 07.00–20.00
Mon–Fri, 08.00–18.00 Sat & Sun (Apr–Sept); 08.00–18.00 daily
(Oct–Mar). The third location is at the cruise terminal. 🅐 Søndre
Akershuskai 🅛 Only open when there is a cruise ship in port.

VisitOslo publishes a guide to Oslo, and a monthly brochure, *What's
On in Oslo*. Here, you will also be able to find good maps of the city
and the transit system. Its website is quite extensive and worth a
look. 🅣 81 53 05 55 🆆 www.visitoslo.com

The city government's offical website offers useful business information in English. ⓦ www.oslo.kommune.no

More politics and business information about the whole country is on the official Norwegian US embassy website. ⓦ www.norway.org

The following website of a commercial hotel booking service also has some tourist information and news features. ⓦ www.oslo.com

Trafikanten can help you with questions about public transport in Oslo and Akershus, and train transport all over eastern Norway. You can telephone its call centre or visit one of its three offices to buy tickets, travel cards and airport transfers and get timetables. Its website also has a useful traffic planner. Its offices are: under the tower in front of Oslo Central Station ⓔ Jernbanetorget 1 ⓛ 08.00–20.00 daily (May–Sept); 07.00–20.00 Mon–Fri, 08.00–18.00 Sat & Sun (Oct–Apr); at Aker Brygge in the waiting room on the quay for the boats to Nesodden ⓔ Stranden 1 ⓛ 07.00–19.00 Mon–Fri, 10.00–18.00 Sat, closed Sun; and between the domestic and international arrivals gates at Gardermoen Airport ⓔ Lufthavnvegen, Gardermoen ⓛ 09.00–18.00 Mon–Sat, 14.00–23.00 Sun ⓣ 177 or 81 50 01 76 ⓦ www.trafikanten.no

Ruter coordinates the different kinds of transport in the Oslo region. Its website has useful maps and information, including a transport map for tourists. ⓦ www.ruter.no

Norwegian Tourist Board Its website is very comprehensive, with lots of practical information. ⓣ 22 00 25 00 ⓦ www.visitnorway.com

Norway Post This paper's website gives up-to-the-minute Norwegian news in English. ⓦ www.norwaypost.no

Emergencies

The following are emergency free-call numbers:
Ambulance & other medical emergencies ❶ 113
Fire ❶ 110
Police ❶ 112
City Police ❶ 22 66 90 50

MEDICAL SERVICES
Doctors
If you become ill or injured while in Norway, your hotel can refer you to a local doctor (most of them speak English). If you are not staying at a hotel, call the national 24-hour emergency medical number ❶ 113

Dentists
Tannlegevakten (❸ Schweigaardsgate 6 ❶ 22 67 30 00
🕐 19.00–22.00 Mon–Fri, 11.00–14.00, 19.00–22.00 Sat & Sun)
is Oslo's public emergency dental clinic in the city centre. On the third floor of Galleriet (Oslo Bus Terminal). No appointments – show up in person. For children and adults. Minimum fee: 467Kr for a ten-minute consultancy.

Hospitals
Oslo kommunale legevakt (Public emergency ward) ❸ Storgata 40
❶ 22 93 22 93 ❾ www.legevakten.oslo.kommune.no 🕐 24 hrs
🚊 Tram: 11, 12, 13, 17 to Hausmanns gate

Pharmacies
Pharmacies are open during normal shopping hours, and some are also open weekends and evenings for emergencies. If you fall

EMERGENCY PHRASES

Help!   Hjelp!   *Yehlp!*

Call an ambulance/Call a doctor/Call the police!
Ring etter en sykebil/Ring en lege/Ring politiet!
Ring ehtterehn sewkerbeel/Ring ehn lehger/Ring pulitee-er!

Can you help me, please?
Kan du hjelpe meg, kanskje?
Kern doo yehlper meh, koonsher?

ill during a trip, the staff at your hotel will normally be able
to direct you to the nearest open pharmacy (*apotek* in Norwegian).
If you use any prescription drugs, be sure to bring enough to last for
your entire stay. Norwegian pharmacies are not permitted to give
out medicine on prescriptions from outside the country, and if you
do run short, you will need to contact a Norwegian doctor in order
to get a prescription for a new supply. There is a 24-hour pharmacy
near the main railway station:
Jernbanetorgets Pharmacy Jernbanetorget 4B 23 35 81 00
www.vitusapotek.no (Norwegian only) 24 hrs T-bane; tram:
11, 12, 13, 17, 18, 19 to Jernbanetorget

POLICE
Oslo District Police Politihuset, Grønlandsleiret 44
02800 or 22 66 90 50 www.politi.no

Lost Property
Police ☎ 22 66 90 50
Trams, buses, T-bane (Oslo Sporveier) ☎ 22 08 53 61
Railway (NSB–Oslo Central Station) ☎ 81 56 83 40

Reporting lost or stolen credit cards:
American Express ☎ 80 03 50 06
Diners Club ☎ 21 01 50 00
Eurocard ☎ 21 01 53 20
Entercard (for Visa and Mastercard) ☎ 21 31 66 00

EMBASSIES & CONSULATES

Australia Embassy The nearest Australia Embassy is in Copenhagen, Denmark. ❸ Dampfaergevej 26, 2nd floor, Copenhagen ☎ +45 70 26 36 76 ⓦ www.denmark.embassy.gov.au

Canada Embassy ❸ Wergelandsveien 7, Oslo ☎ 22 99 53 00 ⓦ www.canadainternational.gc.ca

New Zealand The nearest New Zealand Embassy is in Stockholm, Sweden. ❸ Nybrogatan 11, 3rd floor, Stockholm ☎ +46 84 59 69 40 ⓦ www.nzembassy.com

Republic of Ireland Embassy ❸ Haakon VII's Gate 1, Oslo ☎ 22 01 72 00 ⓦ www.dfa.ie

South Africa Embassy ❸ Drammensveien 88C, Oslo ☎ 23 27 32 20 ⓦ www.saemboslo.no

United Kingdom Embassy ❸ Thomas Heftyes Gate 8, Oslo ☎ 23 13 27 00 ⓦ http://ukinnorway.fco.gov.uk

United States Embassy ❸ Henrik Ibsensgate 48, Oslo ☎ 21 30 85 40 ⓦ http://norway.usembassy.gov

◯ *Magnificent fjord scenery*

ACKNOWLEDGEMENTS

Thomas Cook Publishing wishes to thank the photographers, picture libraries and other organisations, to whom the copyright belongs, for the photographs in this book.

Einar Bog/BigStockPhoto.com, page 49; John Christian/iStockphoto.com, page 113; Dreamstime.com, pages 7 (Norlens), 13 (Isame), 17 (Tyler Olson), 40 (Marco Pitacco), 45 (Goran Bogicevic), 63 (Jrphotography), 96 (Natalia Rumyantseva); epixx/StockXpert.com, page 5; Emanuella Gugnelli/SXC.hu, page 129; Hotel Continental, page 80; Helge Høifødt/Wikimedia Commons, page 85; Stelian Ion/BigStockPhoto.com, page 155; Vegard Bergom Lunde, pages 31, 42 & 68; Per Øyvind Mathisen/BigStockPhoto.com, page 82; Tyler Olson/BigStockPhoto.com, page 32; Oslosurf.com, pages 37, 61, 75, 107; Lisa Govasli Nilsen, page 133; Hugh Shaw/Fotolia.com, page 21; Mari Ringvold Sørli, pages 29, 89 & 111; Stillman Rogers Photography, pages 18, 25, 47, 93, 95, 98, 103, 117, 121, 125 & 141; Bjarte Kvinge Tvedt/SXC.hu, page 130; Ernst Vikne, page 9.

Send your thoughts to
books@thomascook.com

- **Found a great bar, club, shop or must-see sight that we don't feature?**
- **Like to tip us off about any information that needs a little updating?**
- **Want to tell us what you love about this handy little guidebook and more importantly how we can make it even handier?**

Then here's your chance to tell all! Send us ideas, discoveries and recommendations today and then look out for your valuable input in the next edition of this title.

Email the above address (stating the title) or write to:
pocket guides Series Editor, Thomas Cook Publishing, PO Box 227, Coningsby Road, Peterborough PE3 8SB, UK.

WHAT'S IN YOUR GUIDEBOOK?

Independent authors Impartial up-to-date information from our travel experts who meticulously source local knowledge.

Experience Thomas Cook's 165 years in the travel industry and guidebook publishing enriches every word with expertise you can trust.

Travel know-how Thomas Cook has thousands of staff working around the globe, all living and breathing travel.

Editors Travel-publishing professionals, pulling everything together to craft a perfect blend of words, pictures, maps and design.

You, the traveller We deliver a practical, no-nonsense approach to information, geared to how you really use it.

For CAMBRIDGE PUBLISHING MANAGEMENT LIMITED:
Project editor: Karen Beaulah
Layout: Paul Queripel
Proofreaders: Rosalind Munro & Jan McCann

Useful phrases

English	Norwegian	*Approx pronunciation*
BASICS		
Yes	Ja	*Yah*
No	Nei	*Nay*
Please	Vær så snill	*Va sho snil*
Thank you	Takk	*Terk*
Hello	Goddag	*Goud-dahg*
Goodbye	Ha det	*Hah deh*
Excuse me	Unnskyld meg	*Unshewl mey*
Sorry	Beklager	*Beh-klah-gehr*
That's okay	Ingen årsak	*Ing-en or-shahk*
I don't speak Norwegian	Jeg snakker ikke Norsk	*Jai snak-her ik-he Norsk*
Do you speak English?	Snakker du engelsk?	*Snerkur doo ehng-erlsk?*
Good morning	God morgen	*Gou morrgon*
Good afternoon	Goddag	*Goud-dahg*
Good evening	God kveld	*Gou kvehl*
Goodnight	God natt	*Gou nert*
My name is ...	Jeg heter	*Yeh hehterr*
NUMBERS		
One	En	*Ehn*
Two	To	*Too*
Three	Tre	*Treh*
Four	Fire	*Feerer*
Five	Fem	*Fehm*
Six	Seks	*Sehks*
Seven	Sju	*Shoo*
Eight	Åtte	*Otter*
Nine	Ni	*Nee*
Ten	Ti	*Tee*
Twenty	Tjue	*Chewer*
Fifty	Femti	*Fehmti*
One hundred	Hundre	*Hundrer*
SIGNS & NOTICES		
Airport	Flyplass	*Fli-plass*
Railway station	Jernbanestasjon	*Jern-bah-ne-stash-on*
Platform	Plattform	*Plat-form*
Smoking/Non-smoking	Røyk/Ikke-røyk	*Royk/Ik-he royk*
Toilets	Toaletter	*Toa-lett-ehr*
Ladies/Gentlemen	Damer/Herrer	*Dahm-ehr/Hehr-ehr*
Metro/Tram/Bus	T-bane/Trikk/Buss	*Tee-bah-ne/Trikk/Bus*